PHOTOGRAPHY AWARDS

ASSOCIATION OF PHOTOGRAPHERS 2005

ISBN: 0-9543374-6-8

The Association of Photographers
81 Leonard Street, London EC2A 4QS
Tel: +44 (0)20 7739 6669
Fax: +44 (0)20 7739 8707
E-mail: awards@aophoto.co.uk
Website: www.the-awards.com www.image-folio.com   www.the-aop.org

Acting Managing Director   Jonathan Briggs
Awards Manager   Nicola Waterhouse
Publications & Marketing Assistant Rachel Rogers
Colour Consultant   Bob Marchant
Pre-Press, Printing & Binding   Butler and Tanner

CONTENTS

PHOTOGRAPHY AWARDS

The Photography Awards are organised by the AOP, a not-for-profit organisation originally formed in London in 1968 as the Association of Fashion & Advertising Photographers. Today, it brings together professional photographers to protect their rights and promote photography and, as image-makers respond to globalisation, it has members worldwide building an effective network of communications with photographers for the 21st Century.

The images in this book represent some of greatest photographs produced over the last 18 months and include the prestigious AOP Photographers' Awards for AOP members, the new Document category, the AOP Assistants' Awards and the Zeitgeist – a section in which leading industry figures select the images which, for them, sum-up where commercial photography is today.

Whilst the AOP is primarily an organisation for commercial photographers working in the advertising, design, fashion and editorial arenas, our members' work goes far beyond that which appears in public. Professional photographers represent one of the great unsung sources of exceptional creative talent, and contained within these pages is also the personal work of those artists. This is exceptionally pertinent to the creative industries and visual culture today, where the traditional boundaries between commercial and fine art is becoming increasingly less distinct.

So whilst primarily a celebration and recognition of great photographers and their images, it is also a snapshot of our photographic times, judged, curated and compiled by people who are earning their living and care about photography.

The photographic community continually aspires to capture exceptional images and then reproduce them in many innovative and beautiful ways. It is also remarkable to witness how photographers have completely embraced digital capture, manipulation and printing larger digital prints. At EPSON we aim to produce the highest quality photographic output for professional photographers. We do this through the development of our professional photo-inkjet printer range, Ultrachrome inks and range of specialist medias including photo and fine art papers.

We are extremely proud to again be working with the Association of Photographers in producing the Photography Awards 2005. This accolade reinforces the success of our products within the photographic market. Congratulations to all photographers whose work has been included in this book. It is through sharing these innovative and exceptional images with others that makes the subject of photography so rewarding.

EPSON®

AOP PHOTOGRAPHERS' AWARDS

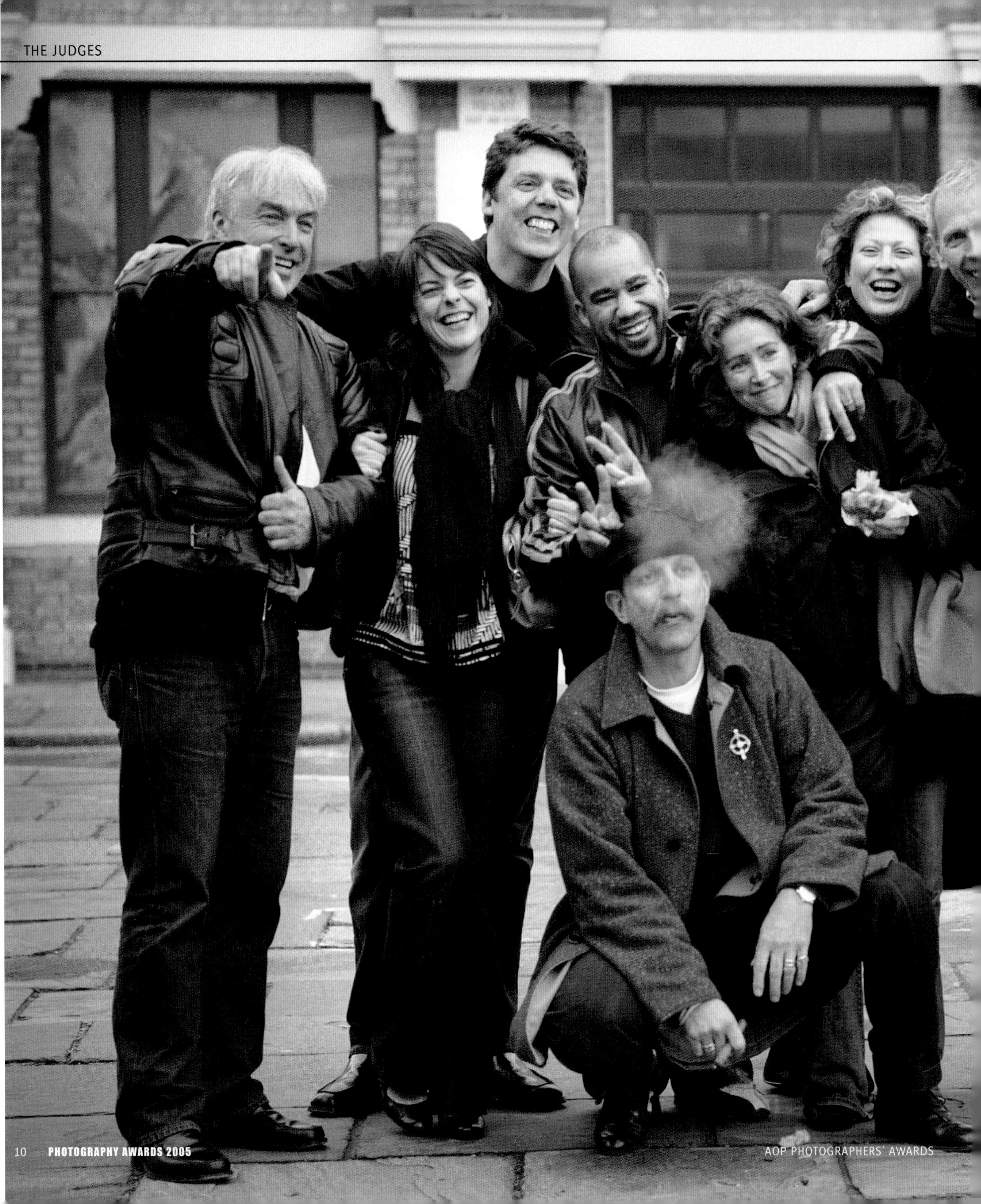

IMAGE © NICK TURPIN

LEFT TO RIGHT: HUGH GILBERT, KELLIE FRENCH, MATTHEW RENTON, ROBERT ALLEN (BACK), MARK GEORGE (FRONT), KARENA PERRRONET-MILLER, MOLLY GODET, PAUL MELLOR, ANTHONY BLAKE

ROBERT **A**LLEN is a London-based fashion photographer who has worked in London and Paris for the last ten years. His editorial clients include Vogue, i-D and Phamous 69. His advertising clients include Free Lance Paris and Fred Perry. His dynamic style also lends itself well to portraiture and he has photographed Naomi Watts and Chris Cunningham, amongst others.

ANTHONY **B**LAKE is a founder member of the AOP. He was an RAF photographer from 1949-54, then freelanced for weddings, press and industry. 1958 saw the first commission for Good Housekeeping followed by a variety of women's magazines doing interiors and rooms sets. In 1959 he started photographing food with Katie Stewart at Woman's Mirror. From 1960 came the first advertising commissions dealing with cars, banks, major industries, cruise lines, champagne, food manufacturers, airlines to name but a few. With 1968 came his first book Time Life in New York, followed by others in the series. The Anthony Blake Photo Library and Gallery was started in the 70s and in 1978 came The Great Chefs of France, followed by about 20 more books over the years. I still press the odd button!

KELLIE **F**RENCH graduated from Edinburgh University in 1997 with an MA in Art History. She joined M&C Saatchi soon afterwards creating a new role for herself as Creative Researcher. Ogilvy & Mather hired her in 2000 to set up a research department where she still currently works scouting for new photographers, illustrators, designers and film makers.

MARK **G**EORGE was born in 1953 in London to a family of architects. He studied furniture design and gained a BA, then became a photographers' agent in 1979 after sharing a Scottish hotel room with a stranger who happened to be a struggling London-based photographer. Mark has worked as an agent out of his Holland Park office ever since.

HUGH **G**ILBERT is an industrial and commercial photographer. His clients include Railtrack companies, TV and film studios, property developers, computer and PR companies. Hugh's personal work includes an on-going series of panoramic images of artists in their studios. This work in progress was shown recently as a solo exhibition at the Royal Academy of Arts.

MOLLY **G**ODET accidentally entered advertising by way of J Walter Thompson where she became incensed at the clumsy way in which men advertised to momen. Having joined McCormick Richards (later to become Publicis) specifically to work on a more female-orientated client list, she won every major advertising prize for her work, amongst other clients, on No7 cosmetics. She has been privileged to work not only with many very famous fashion and beauty photographers, but also with a great many very talented but relatively unknown ones too.

PAUL **M**ELLOR is a London-based photographer who started his career with a press agency in the late 60s. After working for many years in both the advertising and editorial fields, he now concentrates on documentary photography, recording a wide range of social issues in some of the most deprived areas of the world. In the last year he has held exhibitions in London and Boston and has had previous success in both the AOP Awards and the Communication Art Awards in America.

KARENA **P**ERRRONET-**M**ILLER studied history of art, was a painters' assistant, bottle washer, and travelled for years (3rd class) then worked her way up from being a studio sweeper. Loves images, food, music, travel and large cheques.

MATTHEW **R**ENTON is founder of design and branding agency Renton & Johnston based in Chelsea. He was formerly creative director at Corporate Edge where he met business partner Kirsten Johnston. Before that he had been with Michael Peters Limited since 1994. He studied at London College of Printing and Canterbury College of Art. After a number of years working for large agencies, he now enjoys the benefits of running his own business offering creative solutions to a diverse range of clients including Saga, Battersea Dogs Home, Chase Children's Charity and the BBC.

z|e|f|a| images

To inspire ideas, to illustrate stories, and to promote brands and products with the power that goes beyond words, this has been the aim of photography from the beginning.

On this important occasion we congratulate all of the winners – including many partners, both old and new – who so eloquently continue this tradition.

Warmest wishes from the Creative Teams at zefaimages and Corbis.

Lifestyle & Portraiture SINGLE

JIM FENWICK

PRINTER: Jim Fenwick   TITLE: The Blind

NADEGE MERIAU

PRINTER: Jake at Metro Imaging
SYSTEM OPERATOR: Nadege Meriau
STYLING: Mim Quin-Harkin

RABBIT: from Animals Galore
MODEL: Maya

ANDREW PENDLEBURY

PRINTER: Andrew Pendlebury   TITLE: Zak & T
SYSTEM OPERATOR: Andrew Pendlebury

z | e | f | a | images

Lifestyle & Portraiture SERIES

PHILIP LEE HARVEY   **BRONZE**

PRINTER: Gilbert John at Goldenshot
TITLE: Voodoo

COMMISSIONED BY: Caroline Metcalfe
at Conde Nast Traveller
ART DIRECTOR: Pete Winterbottom

ADAM HINTON

PRINTER: Adam Hinton   SYSTEM OPERATOR: Adam Hinton

SIMON THORPE

SYSTEM OPERATOR: Tim at Taylor James

Kodak Professional

As digital imaging continues to change the landscape of photography, the debate continues about how our industry will look in a few years' time. The cynics among us suggest that film will soon be cannibalised by digital, and cast aside completely in favour of more modern technologies.

At Kodak, we recognise that digital is here to stay – however, we do not believe that film and digital are mutually exclusive. We know that as professional photographers you expect the privilege of choice, and we are dedicated to giving you that choice by continuing to develop both film and digital products that will help you produce the highest quality work. Whether you are shooting on film or digitally, whether you are using traditional printing methods or the newest and most innovative, you continue to produce photography that delights the viewer every time.

Kodak is proud to support you through the Association of Photographers and the 2005 Awards. Thank you to all participants for producing consistently outstanding photography.

David Kitchin, Sales & Marketing Manager Kodak Professional.

Fashion & Beauty SINGLE

OLIVIA BEASLEY

CLIENT: Soma Magazine
COMMISSIONED BY: Soma Magazine,
Activism Issue

BRONZE

SYSTEM OPERATOR: Olivia Beasley

TIM FLACH

PRINTER: Stuart Ashton
CLIENT: Getty Images

ART DIRECTOR: Paul Foster
SYSTEM OPERATOR: Tim Flach

FRANK HERHOLDT

PRINTER: Bjarte Rettedal
CLIENT: Grove Magazine
COMMISSIONED BY: Tanya Haughton

ART DIRECTOR: Frank Herholdt
SYSTEM OPERATOR: Bjarte Rettedal

STEVE HOSKINS

PRINTER: Elizabeth Pauthier
CLIENT: 180, Amsterdam
COMMISSIONED BY: Stuart Phillips

ART DIRECTOR: Caprice Yu
SET DESIGN: Model Solutions
PHOTOGRAPH OF YAK: Getty Images /
Adam Crowley

JENS LUCKING

PRINTER: Harry Matthews at Harry's
CLIENT: Stone
ART DIRECTOR: Paul Foster

SYSTEM OPERATOR: Harry Matthews
TITLE: My Muse
MODEL: Alistair Baker

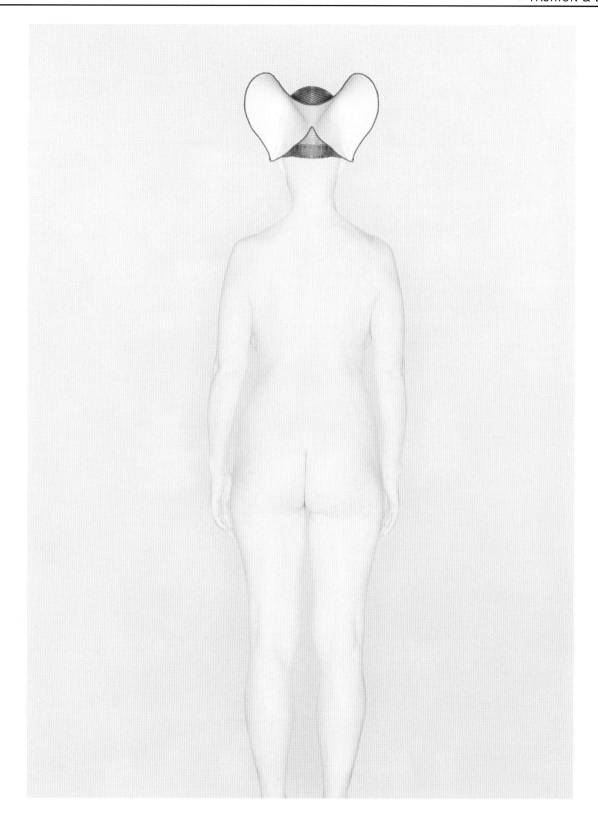

TIM MACPHERSON

PRINTER: Tim MacPherson

DAVID SCHEINMANN

CLIENT: Hewlett Packard
COMMISSIONED BY: Publicis
ART DIRECTOR: Peter Hodgson

MODEL: Raquel Azevedo, Models One
SET: Carmel Said
STYLIST: Desiree Lederer

Kodak Professional

Fashion & Beauty SERIES

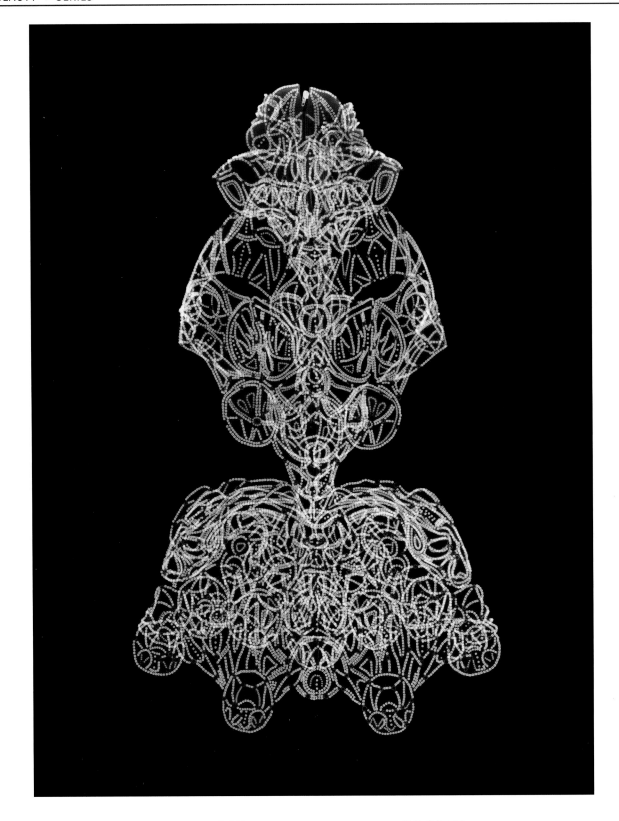

NICK VEASEY

BRONZE

PRINTER: Frame Zero
CLIENT: Alexander McQueen
COMMISSIONED BY:
Michael Nash Associates

ART DIRECTOR: Anthony Michael
SYSTEM OPERATOR: Stuart O'Neill

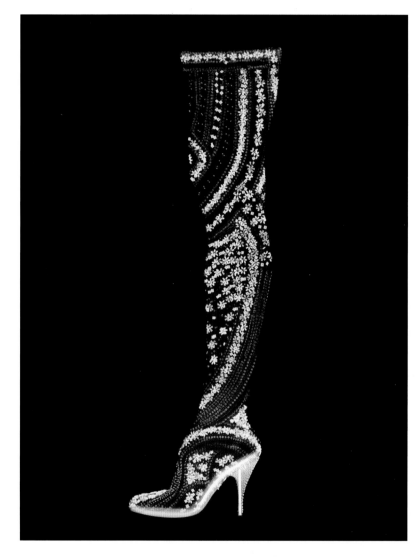

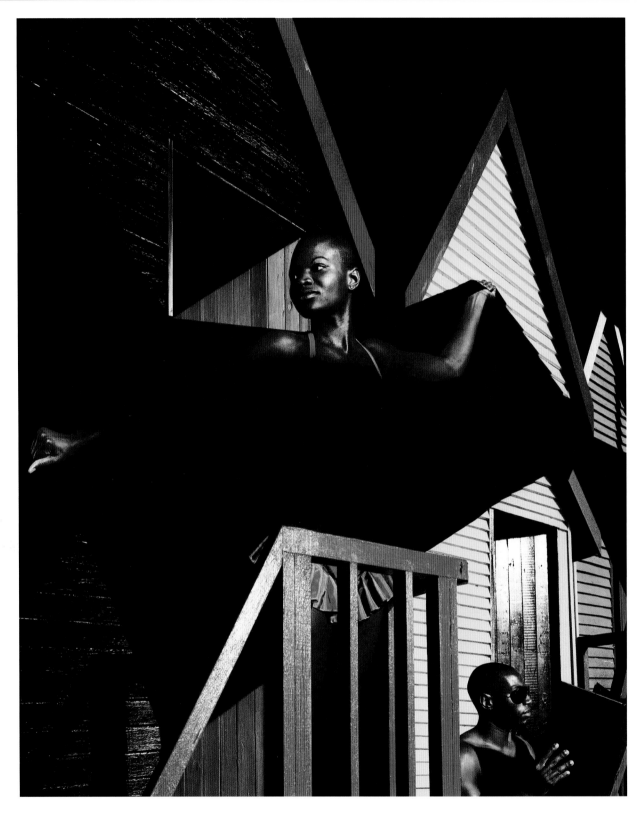

JAAP VLIEGENTHART

BRONZE

PRINTER: Erik Meijer at Souverein
SYSTEM OPERATOR:
Rutger Luÿs at Souverein
TITLE: Coloured

STYLING: Katelyne Verbruggen at
Hoorn / van wegan
HAIR & MAKE-UP: Suzanne Verberk at
Hoorn / van wegan

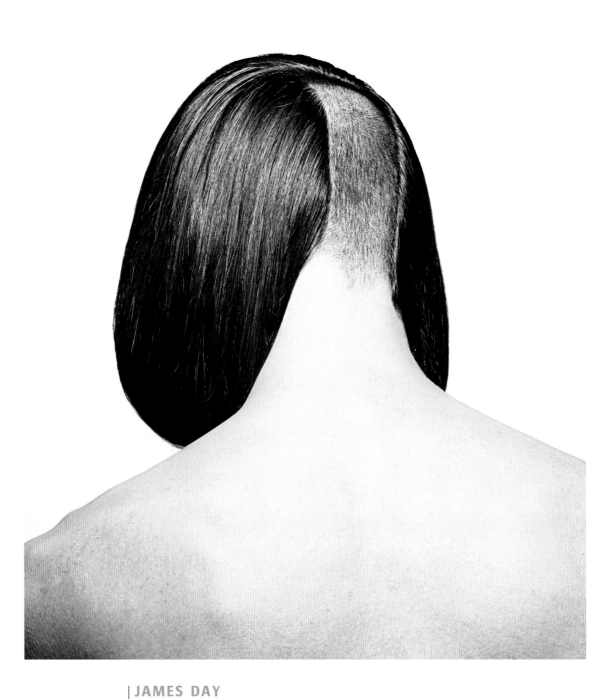

JAMES DAY

ART DIRECTOR: Rhiannon Llewelyn   SYSTEM OPERATOR:
Stuart Calder at Core

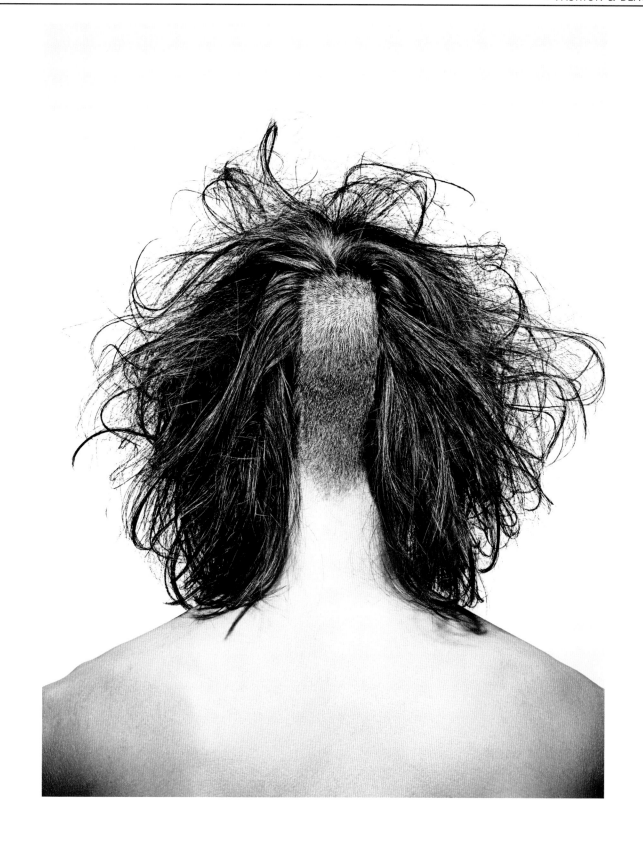

JULIA FULLERTON-BATTEN

Bellagio, Italy

FRANK HERHOLDT

PRINTER: Bjarte Rettedal

ART DIRECTOR: Frank Herholdt
SYSTEM OPERATOR: Clone Creative

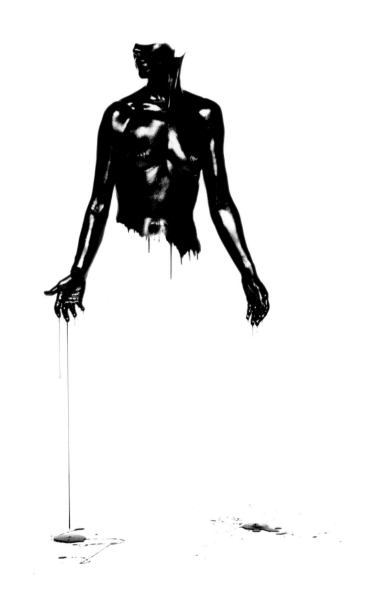

GILES REVELL

PRINTER: Giles Revell
ART DIRECTOR: Giles Revell
SYSTEM OPERATOR: Giles Revell

MAKE-UP ARTIST: Maria Sanchez
MODEL: Anna, Isis Models

Primary are proud to sponsor the prestigious Association of Photographers Awards and to promote the technical and creative excellence in the field of photography.

Digital imaging is playing an increasing role in the world of photography and we would like to thank all our clients for their continual support and encouragement in the successful launch of our digital imaging and printing services over the years. We are delighted to provide a comprehensive range of digital imaging, printing and conventional photographic services.

The Primary team wish to congratulate all the photographers whose work has been acknowledged in the Awards.

Mark Parlett, General Manager, Primary Colour

Landscapes, Interiors & Exteriors SINGLE

CLARISSA LEAHY

PRINTER: Tony Swinney
COMMISSIONED BY: Getty Images

SILVER

ART DIRECTOR: Ashley Jouhar

CHARLIE CRANE

PRINTER: Iris at Bayeux

BRONZE

SYSTEM OPERATOR: Richard Walsh

HENRIK KNUDSEN

TITLE: Lax

BRONZE

FROM THE SERIES: American Pictures

SIMON MCCOMB   **BRONZE**

ART DIRECTOR: Simon McComb   SYSTEM OPERATOR:
TITLE: The Run Shack, Oistins, Barbados   Richard Palmer at The Parlour

JOHN OFFENBACH

Personal work

BRONZE

RICHARD CLARK

ART DIRECTOR: Russ Hodgson

LAURIE HASKELL

PRINTER: Laurie Haskell   CLIENT: Adnams
AD AGENCY: Campbell Doyle Dye

MARKKU LAHDESMAKI

Personal

TOBY MAUDSLEY

PRINTER: Berra at Indigo, Stockholm
CLIENT: RBK / EURO RSCG

COMMISSIONED BY:
Hagströmer & Qviberg
ART DIRECTOR: Mathias Wikstrom

SIMON MILLS

PRINTER: Simon Mills

Landscapes, Interiors & Exteriors SERIES

SIMON WARMER   **SILVER**
PRINTER: Maarten Wouters, Magic   SYSTEM OPERATOR: Peter Witte, Magic

KAI-UWE GUNDLACH

PRINTER: Kai-Uwe Gundlach

kustom

We have pleasure in sponsoring the Still Life category of the AOP Photography Awards and are, as ever, dedicated to supporting the art of the photographer.

Kustom is a company whose passion is the art of creative printing, be it through conventional or digital means, and of developing a close working relationship with our clients. Kustom is a Metro group company so has the benefits of a multi-service parent but with the intimacy and personal touch of a boutique setup. So please do come down for a coffee and chat, meet the people and see the sort of work we do.

Ben Richardson, Managing Director, Metro Imaging.

Still Life SINGLE

TIF HUNTER

PRINTER: Nick Gowler at Taylor James
CLIENT: Nike
COMMISSIONED BY: Wieden &
Kennedy (London)

SILVER

ART DIRECTOR: Lucy Collier
SYSTEM OPERATOR:
Dennis Tufnell at Core
SET BUILD: Metro Models

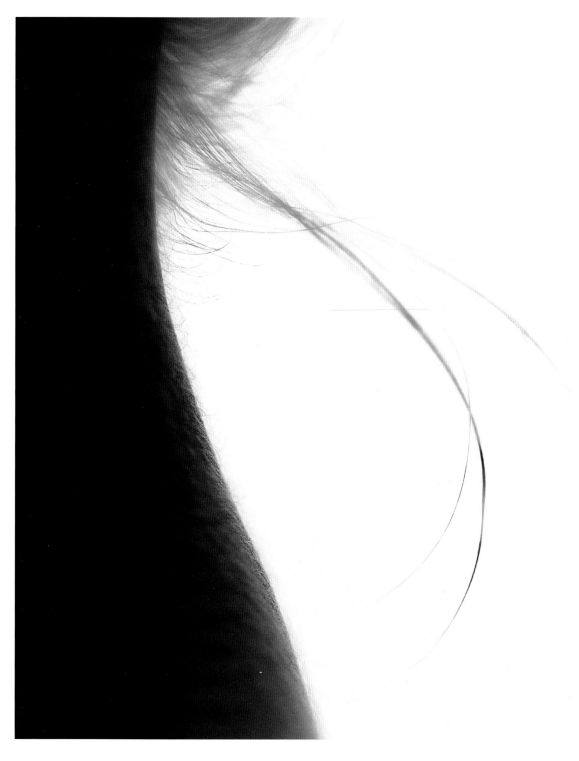

KULBIR THANDI

PRINTER: Kulbir Thandi
MODEL: Natalie Morgan, MOT

BRONZE

PRODUCTION: Shootpeople

ANDY BARTER

CLIENT: Wallpaper*   STYLIST: Roberta Holm

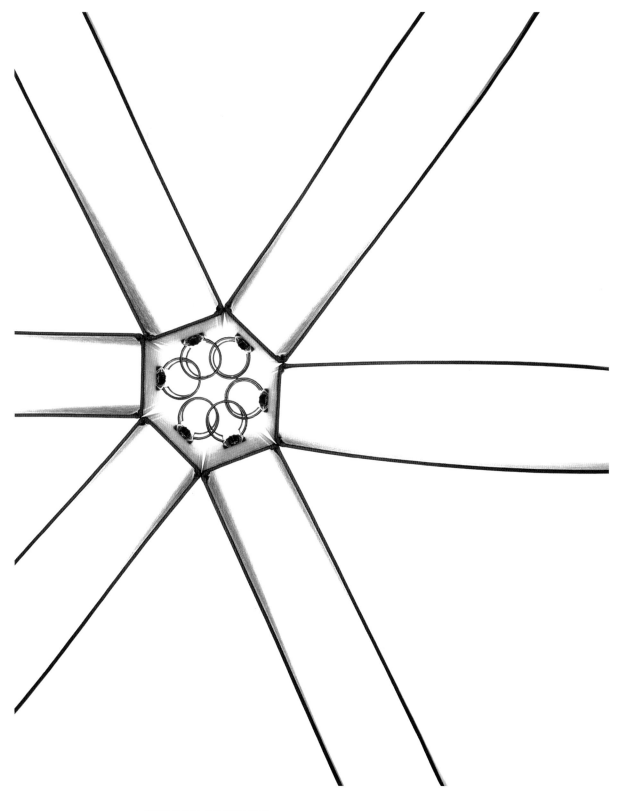

CHIPPY TIFFANY
TITLE: Binders

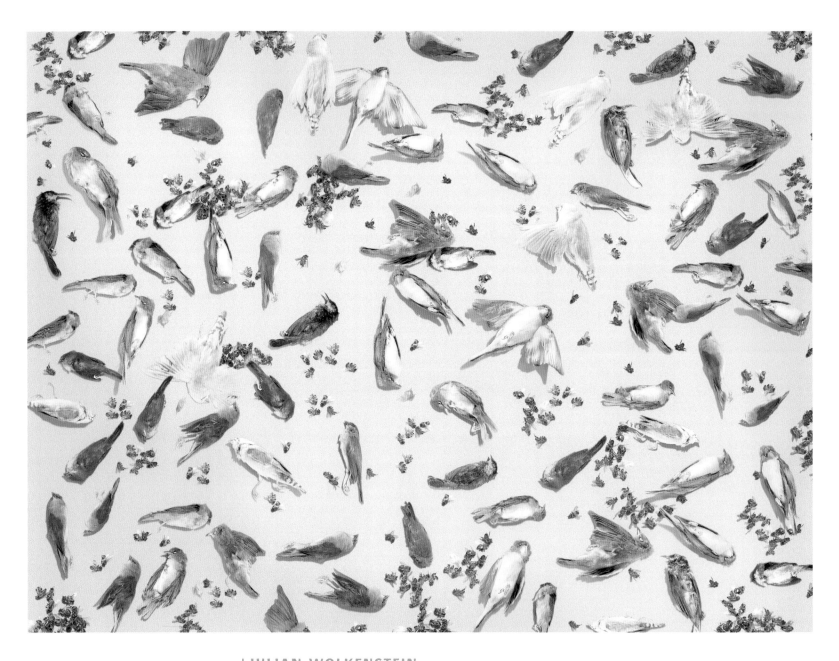

JULIAN WOLKENSTEIN

ART DIRECTOR:
Jan Jacobs / Leo Premutico

SYSTEM OPERATOR:
Julian Wolkenstein
TITLE: Birds & Bees

kustom

Still Life SERIES

GARY BRYAN   BRONZE

PRINTER: SYSTEM OPERATOR:
Tracey Thorne at Big Foot Imaging Brian East at Colourworks

JONATHAN KNOWLES   BRONZE

PRINTER: Jack Lowe

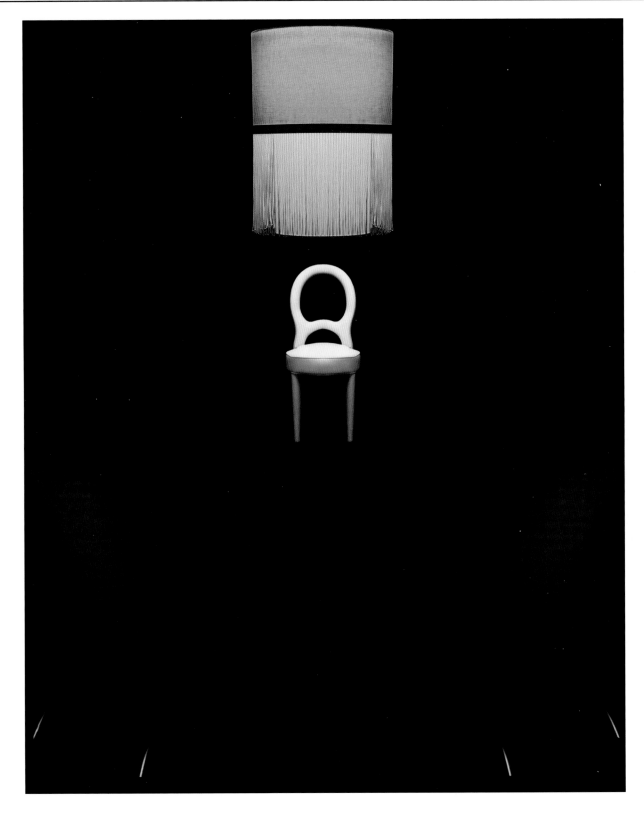

ANDY BARTER

CLIENT: Wallpaper*   STYLIST: Roberta Holm

Chubb Insurance Company of Europe

Chubb Insurance Company of Europe is delighted to sponsor the Portfolio category of the AOP Photographers' Awards. Chubb has proven expertise in insuring photographers and those in film and related industries. We have a long-standing relationship with the Association of Photographers, offering members comprehensive cover for cameras and other equipment, portfolios, props, sets and wardrobe – plus employer's and public liability.

We are designed to be different. We are Chubb Insurance.

Judith Isherwood, European Manager – Chubb Custom Market

Portfolio

CLIENT: IBM COMMISSIONED BY: Wunderman ART DIRECTOR: Dan Badion
SYSTEM OPERATOR: John Offenbach

CLIENT: Hewlett Packard COMMISSIONED BY: Goodby Silverstein & Partners
ART DIRECTOR: Antonio Navas

| JOHN OFFENBACH   SILVER

CLIENT: IBM COMMISSIONED BY: Wunderman ART DIRECTOR: Dan Badion
SYSTEM OPERATOR: John Offenbach

Tokyo, personal work

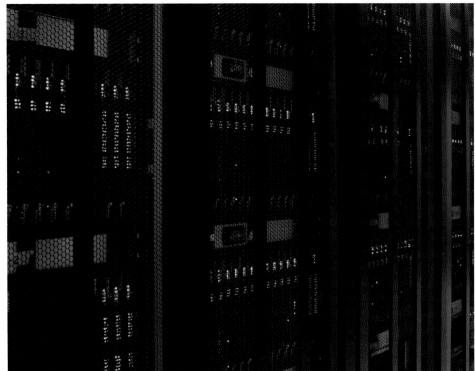

CLIENT: IBM COMMISSIONED BY: Wunderman ART DIRECTOR: Dan Badion

Personal work

CLIENT: IBM COMMISSIONED BY: Wunderman ART DIRECTOR: Dan Badion
SYSTEM OPERATOR: John Offenbach

CLIENT: IBM COMMISSIONED BY: Wunderman ART DIRECTOR: Dan Badion

gettyimages®

Getty Images is proud to sponsor the Association of Photographers, recognising its active role in supporting professional photographers. Congratulations to all of this year's winners.

Project

GEORGE LOGAN **GOLD**

PRINTER: George Logan SYSTEM OPERATOR: George Logan

MORGAN SILK	GOLD
PRINTER: Morgan Silk	SYSTEM OPERATOR: Morgan Silk

TIM SIMMONS

PRINTER: Tim Simmons Studio   TITLE: Intervention
SYSTEM OPERATOR: Tim Simmons Studio

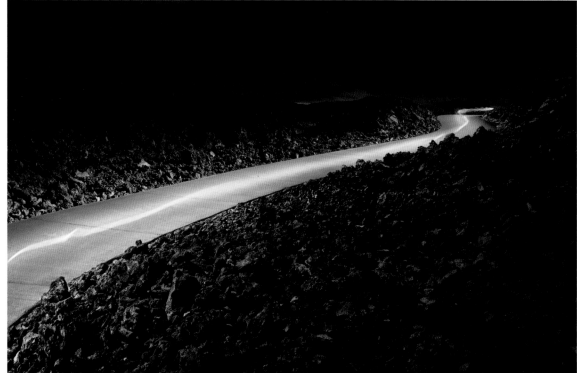

B MA Models wishes to thank all photographers and clients for their continual support and business over 21 years. BMA is the world's only superstore agency, the only all-in-one-call agency.

BMA is proud that all AOP requirements can be sourced at www.bmamodels.com. The source list is endless: twins, triplets, physique & body, hands, legs, feet, characters, actors, hair & make-up artists, kids, brothers & sisters, families, presenters, dancers, and of course model after model, show reels included. Checkout www.bmamodels.com for daily updates.

Judges' Choice

MATT BARLOW

SELECTED BY: Hugh Gilbert

FROM: Landscapes, Interiors & Exteriors single

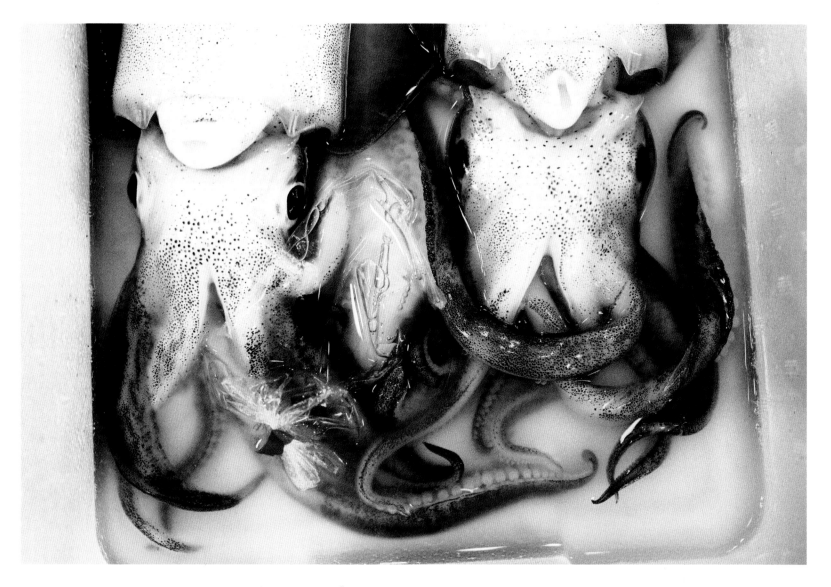

JEAN-LUC BÉNARD

SELECTED BY: Matthew Renton   FROM: Still Life series

SIMON BREMNER

SELECTED BY: Kellie French   FROM: Fashion & Beauty single

NICK GEORGHIOU

SELECTED BY: Anthony Blake   FROM: Fashion & Beauty series

MATT HARRIS

SELECTED BY: Paul Mellor

FROM: Landscapes, Interiors &
Exteriors single

SIMON MILLS

SELECTED BY: Karena Perronet-Miller   FROM: Lifestyle & Portraiture series

KELVIN MURRAY

SELECTED BY: Robert Allen   FROM: Lifestyle & Portraiture single

JOHN PARKER

SELECTED BY: Mark George   FROM: Project

ROBERT WILSON

SELECTED BY: Molly Godet   FROM: Project

PHOTOGRAPHERS' AWARDS

Barlow	Matt	0207 697 8291
Barter	Andy	0207 278 8181
Beasley	Olivia	0207 831 6361
Benard	Jean-Luc	0208 742 3142
Bremner	Simon	07970 181 901
Bryan	Gary	0207 566 1173
Clark	Richard	07973 326 092
Crane	Charlie	07768 633 955
Day	James	0207 739 8985
Fenwick	Jim	07976 292 436
Flach	Tim	0207 613 1894
Fullerton-Batten	Julia	07850 312 083
Georghiou	Nick	0208 995 0611
Gundlach	Kai-Uwe	+49 40 610 189
Harris	Matt	0207 336 0905 agent: 0207 584 0908
Harvey	Philip Lee	agent: 0208 968 9608
Haskell	Laurie	0207 723 3144
Herholdt	Frank	0207 613 3424
Hinton	Adam	0207 486 0999
Hoskins	Steve	0208 740 1115
Hunter	Tif	0207 403 8879
Knowles	Jonathan	0208 741 7577
Knudsen	Henrik	0207 704 6565
Lahdesmaki	Markku	+1 310 456 6964
Leahy	Clarissa	07768 635 330
Logan	George	0207 490 5813
Lucking	Jens	07715 422 444
MacPherson	Tim	0207 370 0712
Maudsley	Toby	agent: 0208 870 3462
McComb	Simon	0207 935 2626
Meriau	Nadege	0207 254 5476
Mills	Simon	0207 241 0088
Murray	Kelvin	0207 431 5414
Offenbach	John	0207 249 4020
Parker	John	0207 229 8882
Pendlebury	Andrew	0115 985 0680
Revell	Giles	0207 278 8818
Scheinmann	David	0207 636 2202
Silk	Morgan	0208 340 7633
Simmons	Tim	0207 729 0234
Thandi	Kulbir	0207 403 0363
Thorpe	Simon	07966 261 532
Tiffany	Chippy	07850 540 701
Veasey	Nick	01622 737 722
Vliegenthart	Jaap	+31 (0)20 411 7735
Warmer	Simon	+31 (0)20 692 3955
Wilson	Robert	0207 263 9901
Wolkenstein	Julian	07748 735 858

AOP Document

ALL IMAGES © NICK TURPIN

BETWEEN THE WORKS OF ART... ADRIAN EVANS (LEFT) AND HOMER SYKES

BEHIND THE LINES: ZED NELSON

FROM THE BACK OF THE BUS... PAUL REAS, LEE MARTIN AND JON LEVY

JON **L**EVY started his career in photography at the ICP in NY where he completed the documentary and photojournalism certificate programme in 1989. After a brief stint in the UK freelancing for the Independent, he returned to NY to work with Gamma Liaison agency. Levy spent ten years covering news and feature work in the US for Gamma Liaison and later for Agence France Presse, the wire service, for whom he became a staff photographer. Returning to UK in 1999, Levy built on the success of foto8.com, an internet photo-journal he had begun in Brooklyn amongst professional photographers by launching EI8HT magazine in print. Now in its third year, EI8HT is sold in over 15 countries.

ADRIAN **E**VANS Director, Panos Pictures, studied History and History of Art at York University. After graduation he drifted through many jobs ranging from counting chickens to bicycle couriering. Having always been interested in photography he took a job as a picture researcher in a small photo agency and three years later he moved on to run Panos Pictures – at that time a small photo agency specialising in the environment. After five years of expansion he bought a controlling share in the agency. Since then, Panos has grown to become one of the leading photojournalism agencies in the world.

LEE **M**ARTIN joined Getty Images as Vice-President for the News & Sport business in February 1998 having previously been the UK Joint Managing Director for Allsport which was acquired by Getty Images. Lee, amongst other responsibilities for Getty Images, owns the relationships with its sports leagues and governing bodies in EMEA. Lee has covered, in a professional working capacity, ten winter and summer Olympic Games – Sarajevo in 1984 being his first and Athens 2004 his most recent. Lee sits on a number of sports industries working partys and has judged many of the world's most prestigious sports photographic competitions.

ZED **NELSON** is best known for his project 'Gun Nation' which has been published as a book and exhibited worldwide. Nelson has won many of photography's top awards, including a First Prize in the World Press Photo Competition, Visa d'Or for Best Magazine Feature of the Year at the International Festival of Photojournalism, France, the Alfred Eisenstaedt Award for photojournalism, USA, and First prize in the NikonAwards (UK).

PAUL **REAS** was born in Bradford West Yorks. He studied Documentary Photography at Newport College, Gwent from 1982-84. Throughout the 1980s and 1990s he worked regularly for magazines such as The Sunday Times, The Observer and the Independent. His two books 'I Can Help' and 'Flogging A Dead Horse' were published by Cornerhouse. He has exhibited extensively in the UK and abroad, including shows at The Photographers Gallery, The Barbican and The Netherlands Photo Institute. He has taught at various photography courses across the country: Newport, Farnham, LCP and Brighton. He currently lives in Brighton where his time is divided between working commercially on advertising campaigns and making personal work.

HOMER **SYKES** is a well-known independent photographer, based in London. He has worked in the corporate and editorial field for over 30 years. He is the author of numerous books. In 2002 he set up a one-man-band publishing company called Mansion Editions (www.mansion editions.com). On the Road Again and Hunting with Hounds were the first two books that he has self-published. He thoroughly recommends the roller coaster self-publishing challenge.

News SINGLE

Panic outside the British consulate in Istanbul, Turkey, minutes after it was destroyed by a car bomb in November 2003. Twenty-seven people were killed and over 450 injured in simultaneous attacks on the consulate and HSBC offices, blamed on Turkish militants linked to al Qaeda.

| GEORGE GEORGIOU

The Queen peers around a corner during an official tour of the newly redeveloped Royal Albert hall.

RICHARD POHLE

CLIENT: *The Times*
COMMISSIONED BY: *The Times*

A woman dressed in a burka casts her vote in a polling booth in Lame Ya E Shahid High School in Kabul during the historic Presidential Election in Afghanistan.

RICHARD WAINWRIGHT
CLIENT: Corbis

AOP Document

News SERIES

Attack on Monrovia, Liberia, June 2003. A secretive rebel group, Liberians United for Reconciliation and Democracy (LURD), began their final assault on the city of Monrovia. Their stated aim was to remove President Charles Taylor from power. I was the only photographer to work behind rebel lines during these attacks.

| TIM A HETHERINGTON   SILVER

JONATHAN OLLEY   BRONZE
Self-assigned project

'Devil's Garden'. Unexploded ordnance (UXO), a legacy of money, power, violence and death in Iraq, 2004.

DARIO MITIDIERI
Self-assigned, published as eight-page feature in *Paris Match*

An estimated 300,000 people disappeared in Iraq during Saddam Hussein's brutal regime. In April 2003, thousands of Iraqi people began what was referred to as 'the circuit of pain', criss-crossing Iraq and visiting mass graves, with the hope of identifying the remains of their missing relatives. The photographs are part of the series 'Mass graves of Iraq', awarded 3rd place in general news stories – World Press Photo 2004.

Sport SINGLE

DAVID GRAY
CLIENT: Reuters News Agency

DAVID GRAY
CLIENT: Reuters News Agency

DAVID GRAY
CLIENT: Reuters News Agency

DAVID GRAY
CLIENT: Reuters News Agency

DAVID GRAY
CLIENT: Reuters News Agency

Off and Paddling (2004 Athens Olympic Games, K4 Men's Final)

LEO MASON

CLIENT: *Time* Magazine
COMMISSIONED BY: *Time* Magazine International

LARS MOELLER

CLIENT: BT (daily newspaper, Denmark)
COMMISSIONED BY: BT

AOP Document

Sport SERIES

| CHRIS DE BODE   BRONZE

The world of cycle racing extends far beyond the Tour de France. These pictures were taken in Colombia, Cuba, Qatar and Senegal, just four of the diverse stops on the international circuit. From rutted roads to civil war, nothing is allowed to get in the way of the race.

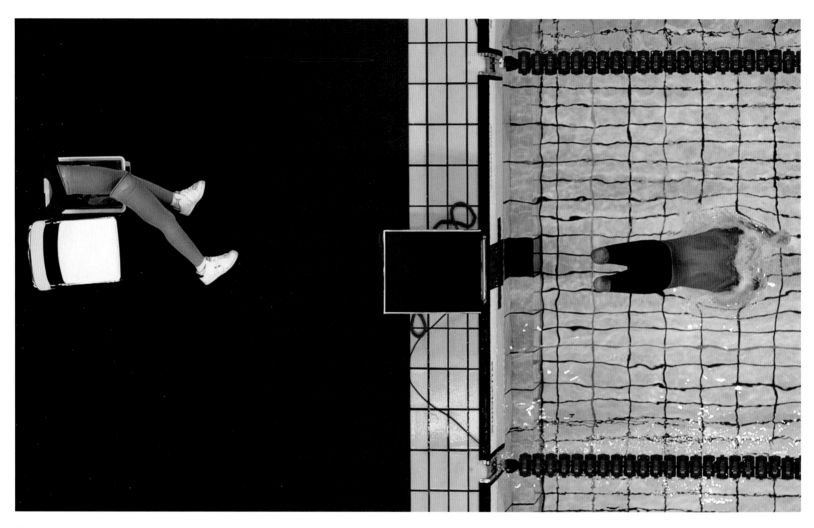

The Paralympic Games are the Olympics for athletes with physical disabilities, held in Athens, Greece from 17 to 28 September 2004. Four thousand athletes participated, representing 145 countries in 19 sports. The swimming competition was the most inspirational yet humbling assignment I have ever experienced as a photographer.

BOB MARTIN   **BRONZE**

CLIENT: *Sports Illustrated*
COMMISSIONED BY: Steve Fine, Director of Photography

Feature SINGLE

Taken from feature story Crack Unlimited/Street Pastors. Gun crimes have tripled in London during the past two years and there has been a rapid increase in teenagers purchasing guns, such that they appear to have become a fashion accessory. Street pastors have been given lectures on the subject of firearms, provided by the officers from the SO19 squad of the Metropolitan Police. Brixton, London, April 2004.

| DEJAN KOSTIC   BRONZE

| MARY-JANE MAYBURY   BRONZE

GARY CALTON
Forms part of a story of Japanese Street Culture, 'Japanese-Style Western Things'

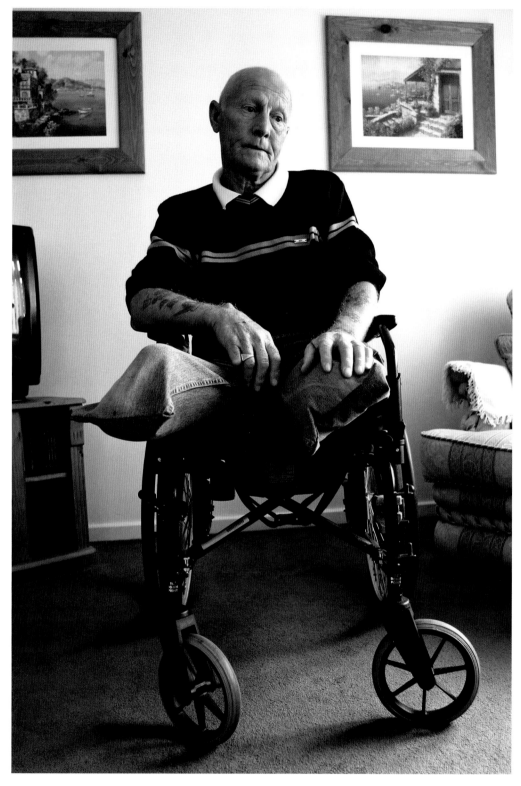

Retired builder Ken Holder, 60, in the wheelchair he is confined to after catching the hospital superbug MRSA, leaving him in a condition where he is unable to use prosthetic limbs. Ken still has the bug but refuses to allow any more to be amputated from his legs. 23 July 2003.

LEWIS WHYLD

COMMISSIONED BY: *The Daily Express*

Feature SERIES

JONATHAN OLLEY   SILVER

Self-assigned project

Canute's Island (Sea defences of the British Isles). Twenty-eight per cent of the UK coastline constitutes a sea wall. Global warming and land settlement is causing the sea to encroach upon our tiny island once more. Should we retreat from the sea, or find the money for elaborate engineering solutions?

CHRIS ANDERSON

COMMISSIONED BY: *The Times* Magazine

Players' Ball, Chicago. East of the Ryan Motel, Chicago's Southside, home to an annual gathering of the nation's Pimps and Players. As the industry moves onto the internet, these old school players find their particular brand of pimping marginalised, as they try to hang onto a business model, and sense of style, that had its heyday in the `70's.

| HEIDI BRADNER

The Nenets people are nomadic Siberian reindeer herders. Their lives are intertwined with the lives of their animals, which provide transport, clothing, shelter and food as they cross the Arctic tundra. 'For us, deer is wealth. Without them we are nothing, we cannot survive,' says one herder.

| MICHAEL CLEMENT

Daily life SINGLE

A boy ponders his father's artificial legs. The man was a victim of the RUF rebels' attempt to terrorise the civilian population by mutilations and killings. Makeni, Sierra Leone 2004..

STUART FREEDMAN   BRONZE

CLIENT: *Guardian* Weekend Magazine
COMMISSIONED BY: Handicap International

Kadiatu and her grandchild just before their afternoon nap. Kadiatu had both legs cut off by rebels in Freetown. She was 'adopted' by a Sierra Leonian woman in the USA and lived there for several months but decided to return to her family. Amputees Resettlement Village, Hastings, Sierra Leone, 2004.

STUART FREEDMAN

CLIENT: *Guardian* Weekend Magazine
COMMISSIONED BY: Handicap International

Tibet. A peaceful culture that was destroyed by Chairman Mao's ruthless colonialists. 10,000 monasteries were ransacked and pillaged. Now there are still remote villages where cultural traditions continue to survive. In the village of Labrang, monks sit through a snow blizzard to attend a Debate in the presence of the Living Buddha.

| JEREMY HUNTER

Azahir Adam Harun, 12, in the school at Ardamatta camp, Darfur. Azahir fled her village when it was attacked by Janjaweed militants in January 2004. 'My previous school was better than this one,' she says. 'I had plenty of friends there. I don't know where any of them went. I'm very worried about them.'

CAROLINE IRBY

COMMISSIONED BY: Save the Children, US

Daily life SERIES

| CHRIS ANDERSON & ALISON LOCKE

Photographed at Brockwell lido over August Bank Holiday 2004, the project is a document of inner city daily life through portraits of the people using this local amenity. Questions of place and identity are raised by photographing these people against a backdrop that transports them out of this everyday context.

JOHN ANGERSON

Personal project

The Jesus Army has various 'membership styles' one of the first is 'new birth' with a baptism in a large pool inside the marquee (top left). Shadows cast on the street of Leeds Yorkshire, England, during recruitment week (bottom left). Members from the 'Crown of Life' community house, Sheffield, travel across South Yorkshire and hold smaller mid week neighbourhood home "cell" group worship often in residential houses, like this one in Barnsley (top). Jesus Fellowship elder (left) Jack Sutcliffe facilitates the Baptistism of Iranian Asylum seeker 'Ali' in the cold waters of the River Wharf North Yorkshire England. Afghan Asylum seeker 'Zorhab' (right) helps in the re-birth ceremony. Many persecuted Christians from across the globe have found refuse in the Jesus Army (above).

JONATHAN OLLEY

Self-assigned project

Explosive Ordnance Disposal under the auspices of the UN, contracts have been awarded to private companies (in this case Zimbabwean) to aid the clear-up of over a million tonnes of high-explosive munitions that currently litter the Iraqi landscape

KIRAN RIDLEY
CLIENT: Orbis

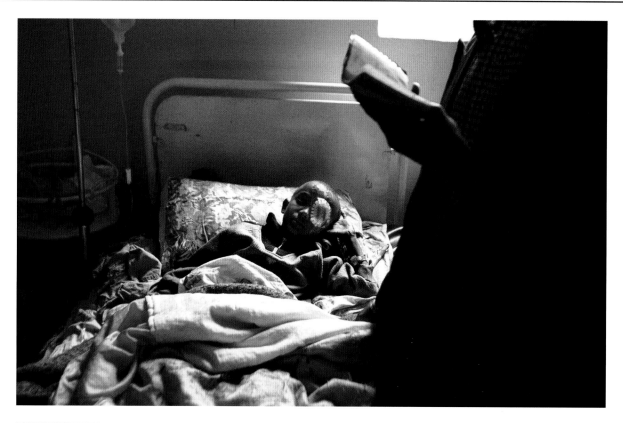

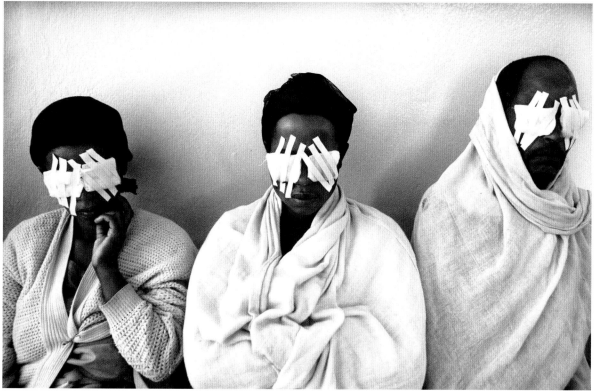

Blindness in Ethiopia, has enormous personal and social costs. Over 1 million of 67 million are blind and 3 million visually impaired, almost double that of other developing nations. Eighty per cent are preventable or treatable, cured by simple and inexpensive surgery, but in one of the world's poorest countries even the most basic medical help is often out of reach. Blindness or poor vision can mean never going to school, never marrying and always feeling a burden.

ALIKI SAPOUNTZI

Personal Work

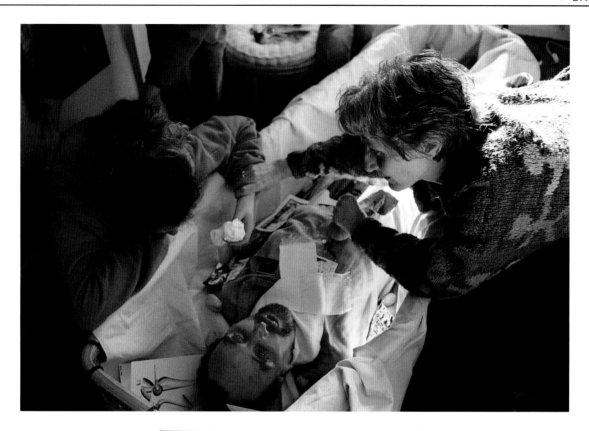

Frankie called me one day to find out whether I would go to Devon to take a family portrait. This I happily did. We all knew he was going to die of Leukaemia soon, but he didn't look like a dying man. Two weeks later his wife called as he was breathing his last breaths, inviting me to join them. I flew in, hours after his departure. His presence, still palpable, in the room. Whilst supporting his family, it felt crucial to capture the moment.

Anderson	Chris	07930 404 932
Angerson	John	07767 822 828
Bradner	Heidi	agent: 0207 234 0010
Calton	Gary	07050 107 626 agent: 0207 739 9000
Clement	Michael	07976 216 050
De Bode	Chris	agent: 0207 234 0010
Freedman	Stuart	07831 505 514
Georgiou	George	agent: 0207 234 0010
Gray	David	+61 29 373 1808
Hetherington	Tim A	07767 785 318
Hunter	Jeremy	07768 490 907 / 01780 410 600
Irby	Caroline	07967 659 043
Kostic	Dejan	07967 502 806 / 0207 488 4002
Locke	Alison	07966 483 556
Martin	Bob	07785 233 255
Mason	Leo	07831 467 926 / 0208 748 1302
Maybury	Mary-Jane	07810 650 278
Mitidieri	Dario	agent: 0207 262 1774
Moeller	Lars	+45 20 113 322
Olley	Jonathan	07973 893 691
Pohle	Richard	0208 393 8946 / 07850 947 132
Ridley	Kiran	07971 287 183
Sapountzi	Aliki	0131 229 0951
Wainwright	Richard	07797 718 769
Whyld	Lewis	07815 820 323

IMAGE © NICK TURPIN

SOCIAL HOUSING IN EASTERN EUROPE

would like to explain a little bit about why I think this project came about. It is my dream project in two ways. First, I have always been interested in notions of 'home', what it means to be home, to have a home. Much of my work is based around this theme. And secondly, Eastern Europe – my life long, somewhat naïve fascination with eastern Europe. My childhood hero was Nadia Comaneci, and I felt devastated and cheated that I had not been born in Romania, but rather a far-distant Australia.

My cousin was born the daughter of an Albanian refugee and named Tirane after the capital of their former home. One of the first places I travelled to upon arriving in Europe was East Berlin where I saw eastern block housing for the first time. I hitch-hiked with a convoy of Iranian truck drivers though Bulgaria and Yugoslavia, really just catching a glimpse out the window. This list is just to say that my interest in eastern Europe is long felt.

My work involves photographing social housing in capital cities in eastern Europe. Social housing is housing intended for households with a relatively low income. All over Europe, the three basic criteria of social housing and housing policy are affordability, accessibility and quality. Affordable housing can contribute to economic stability and has a crucial role in promoting social integration. It is of the highest importance for newly emerging countries.

The last decade in Europe brought substantial changes in the housing sector, particularly to countries in transition. The scope and impact of these changes has never been experienced before in Europe. Some of the outcomes have had a negative impact on social stability and the meeting of elementary human needs.

My primary interest lies with Eastern Europe where many state-owned blocks of flats have been returned to their previous owners or their descendants by restitution laws. Lack of housing is, of course, most severe in big cities where populations are greatest. By photographing social housing dwellings in these capitals we can draw a picture of how the emerging Europe is catering for its poorest citizens.

ZEITGEIST

When you look at the Zeitgeist in 50 years' time, you should get a sense of the values and philosophies that drive us.

When looking at Zeitgeist, the question we should be asking is: 'Is it fresh?'
You want people to come up with a freshness in one way or another, a new way of doing things. They are pictures that in a sense are going to be copied. Will somebody want to copy this? Will someone want to take it home and use it as a reference? That is the essence of the Zeitgeist.

ZEITGEIST

MOT MODELS

In the year that we celebrate our 20th birthday, MOT Models is proud and honoured to have been invited to sponsor the AOP Awards for a sixth consecutive time.

Over the years, we may have grown quite a bit, but we still aim to provide a friendly, efficient, fair and affordable service to all of our customers, who have included almost all of the major photographers and advertisers in the UK and many in Europe and the USA.

2005 has seen us open an office in London and we will endeavour to use this to provide you with an even better service in town.

Whatever else has changed, our objective remains the same – to make your assignment a success.

JOHN **HEGARTY** *Chairman & Worldwide Creative Director, BBH*
John started in advertising as a junior Art Director at Benton and Bowles, London in 1965. He almost finished in advertising, 18 months later, when they fired him. He joined a small Soho agency, John Collings & Partners, going places. They did – out of town.

In 1967, he joined the Cramer Saatchi consultancy which became Saatchi & Saatchi in 1970, where he was a founding shareholder. One year later he was appointed Deputy Creative Director.

John left in 1973 to co-found TBWA, London as Creative Director. The agency was the first to be voted *Campaign*'s (the UK's leading advertising magazine), Agency of the Year in 1980. He left in 1982 to start Bartle Bogle Hegarty. Four years later, in 1986, BBH was also voted *Campaign* magazine's Agency of the Year, and won the title once again for 1993. In addition, BBH became the Cannes Advertising Festival's very first Agency of the Year in 1993 by winning more awards than any other agency. It also won the title again in 1994. At the end of 2003, BBH was also awarded Agency of the Year by *Marketing and Media* and *Marketing Europe*.

John's credits include 'Vorsprung Durch Technik' for Audi, and Levi's 'Bath' and 'Launderette'. His awards include two D&AD Golds and six Silvers, Cannes Golds and Silvers, and

British Television Gold and Silvers. More recently, he was awarded the D&AD President's Award for outstanding achievement in the advertising industry and chaired the 1999 New York Art Directors' Advertising Show.

John is BBH's Chairman and Worldwide Creative Director.

ALL IMAGES © NICK TURPIN

MICHAEL **D**ENNY, *Director, Roundel.* Michael started his career working for the UK Central Office of Information, providing design advice to various government agencies. He went on to head up various creative departments in a number of design and advertising agencies before being appointed Creative Director of Roundel in 1982. Mike led the management buy-out of Roundel in the late 1980s forming one of the UK's most successful independent design groups.

Over the last 20 years, his graphic and branding work has won many awards in the UK, mainland Europe, the Far East and the USA. He was voted on the board of the leading industry professional body, British Design and Art Direction (D&AD) and was subsequently asked to chair its corporate branding sub-committee. He has also sat on, and chaired, many international design juries.

< **S**AMANTHA **T**HOMAS is *Editorial Director of Network Photographers,* an independent London-based photographic agency, internationally renowned for its reportage and documentary photography.

Samantha has been Picture Editor of three international picture agencies, starting out at Camera Press and then moving to Sygma, prior to joining Network in August 2001.

At Camera Press, an agency producing a broad spectrum of stories, she began her career as a journalist, before moving onto the picture desk as a junior researcher and editor. In just over a year, Samantha was appointed Picture Editor, responsible for news and features, a role she continued until she joined the French news agency, Sygma, where she ran the London picture desk.

'The 'real woman' issue has created a huge debate – and at last the cosmetics industry
is not just using models like Kate Moss. It is a genuine reflection of what people feel about beauty.
It's undoubtedly the advertising image of the year.' John Hegarty

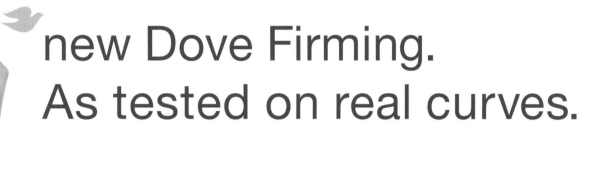

new Dove Firming.
As tested on real curves.

Dove
Firming Range

Dove
Body Firm
Intensive
Firming
Gel Cream

Dove
Body Firm
Firming
Body Wash

Dove
Body Firm
Firming
Lotion

Photographer: Rankin; Art Director: Joerg Herzog; Copywriter: Dennis Lewis; Creative Director: Dennis Lewis / Malcolm Poynton;
Typographer: Sid Tomkins; European Client Services Director: Daryl Fielding

Photographer: Ashton Keiditsch; Agency: VCCP; Client: O_2; Art Director: Mark Orbine; Copywriter: John McLaughlin; Retouch: Stanley's Post

'There is something about this kind of humanising of technology that O$_2$ has captured. It has been made powerful by the imagery used and the way it has been done. I sense an optimism that somehow society needs to reflect on. You will look back in five years' time and think that was 2004. It succeeds becuase of the craft and the way that it has tried to make technology more appealing.' John Hegarty

iPod Silhouettes Creative Director: Duncan Milner/Eric Grunbaum; Art Director: Susan Alinsangan;
Photographer/Illustrator: Matthew Welch

'It's very iconic – it's amazing that they are actually photographs.
When I found out I was quite surprised – I was convinced it was illustration.' John Hegarty

'These adverts are very reminiscent of the 1960s but with a modern slant which makes them so effective.' Mike Denny

iPod Silhouettes Creative Director: Duncan Milner/Eric Grunbaum; Art Director: Susan Alinsangan;
Photographer/Illustrator: Matthew Welch

iPod Silhouettes Creative Director: Duncan Milner/Eric Grunbaum; Art Director: Susan Alinsangan;
Photographer/Illustrator: Matthew Welch

'Fashion for Walls personalises
the matter of home decoration
and really appeals to the vanity of
people, bearing in mind the fact that
women tend to lead on decorating
the home.' Samantha Thomas

Photographer: Christophe Gilbert; Retoucher: Yanick Le Coq (Saga CG); Agency: TBWA, Brussels; Creative Director: Jan Macken;
Art Director: Michaël Mikiels; Copywriter: Karl Hansenne

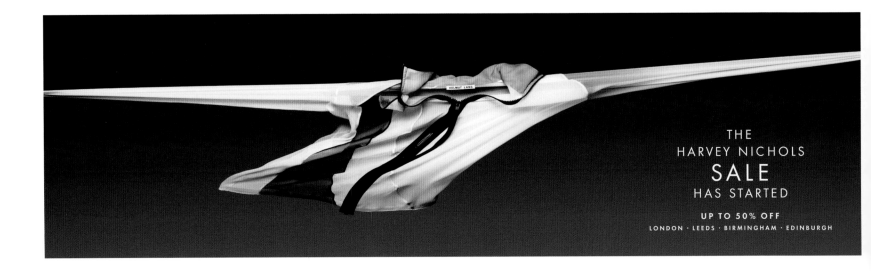

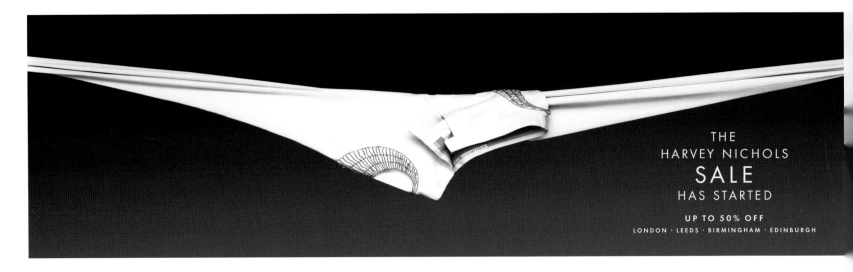

'Just like the success of the Dove advert, the Harvey Nichols
sales series tells you a lot about brand presentation.
And it's fresh.' Mike Denny

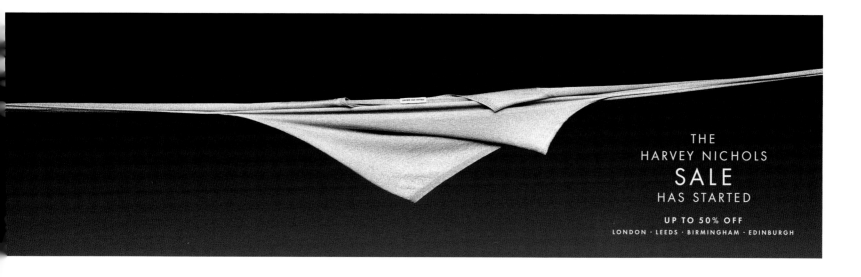

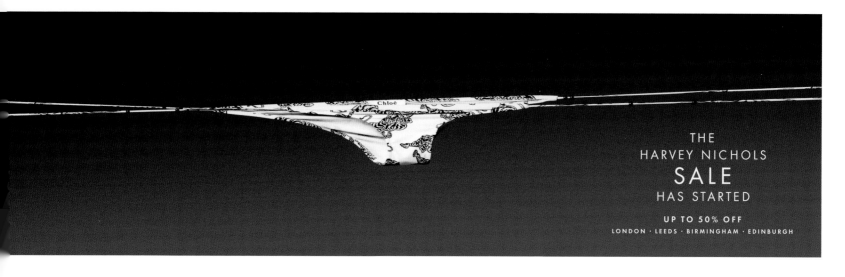

Photographer: Paul Zak; Agency: DDB London; Art Directors: Justin Tindall & Adam Tucker

Client: Directorate of Naval Recruiting; Agency: Rainey Kelly Campbell Roalfe / Y&R; Photographer: Conor Masterson;
Art Director: Jason Stewart; Copywriter: Brian Cooper; Retouching: Mark Kendrick @ Actis

Agency: Miles Calcraft Briginshaw Duffy; Photographer: Alan Mahon; Art Buyer: Cara Devenish;
Art Director: Dave Hobbs; Writer: Richard Stoney; Designer: Kerry Roper; Creative Directors: Paul Briginshaw & Malcolm Duffy

'Stop the guns is a very modern image. It's all about your interaction with violence, and stopping it with your mobile phone. The fact that your phone could stop violence makes it work.' John Hegarty

'I think it reflects a lot of issues around our time which are very relevant. They are now... using Nokia, linking the guns to the gadget culture that to me is our time.' Samantha Thomas

'We are living in an agressive time and these are quite aggressive images, particularly the aircraft carrier. If I was a boy, playing with toys, I think it would strike a chord.' Mike Denny

'The pictures grab your attention – mixing the computer games idea with reality communicates that you can be part of this.' Samantha Thomas

IF ONLY
EVERY CHILD WAS
BORN WITH A
SILVER
SPOON

If only poverty didn't crush the hope and joy of thousands of children in the UK every year. If only poverty didn't rob them of the chance of a positive future. If only there was no such thing as poverty. Then there would be no need for Barnardo's to use shocking images. There would be no need for us to ask you to call 0800 032 7222 now. There would be no need for Barnardo's to exist. If only. www.barnardos.org.uk

Barnardo's
GIVING CHILDREN BACK THEIR FUTURE

THERE ARE NO
SILVER SPOONS
FOR CHILDREN BORN INTO
POVERTY

Baby Mary is three minutes old. Thanks to poverty she faces a desperate future. Poverty is waiting to crush Mary's hope and ambition and is likely to lead her to a future of drug abuse. We can't end poverty but we can provide the practical skills that Mary and thousands of others in the UK need to stop it predetermining their lives. Don't let poverty destroy a future. Call us on 0800 032 7222 or visit www.barnardos.org.uk now.

Barnardo's
GIVING CHILDREN BACK THEIR FUTURE

Creative Directors: Adrian Rossie & Alex Grieve; Art Director & Copywriter: Johnny Leathers & George Prest; Photographer: Miles Aldridge

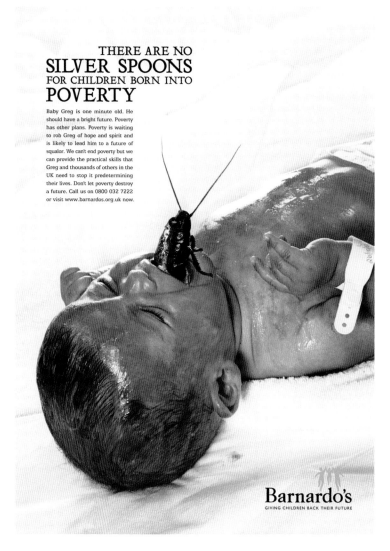

'It's a shame that these were banned. I understand with commercial images that
if you are selling a car that they may say this is not is good taste – but we are not selling a
product, we are trying to save children from an appalling future. it's not Benetton trying to
sell you a jumper.' John Hegarty

'This captures a dream-like feeling. The "I don't want to be here" sense. It creates a lovely escapism, as opposed to showing you some white snow. It has that lovely incidental nature that you might be driving along and just happen to see something...' John Hegarty

Your grip on snow can be better than your grip boots and bindings that flex for maximum accelera

ATOMIC

Photographer: William Huber; Photo composite: William Huber; Art Director: Keith Manning;
Copywriter: Ariel Broggi; Creative Director: Brian Goss; Agency: Nail Communications, Providence RI, USA

We see it too.

h the Atomic R:EX Ride System: skis,
rol. Obsession? Compulsion? Addiction?

Creative Director: Mark Reddy; Creative Team: Grant Parker, Patrick McClelland; Photographer: Tim Bret Day; Retoucher: Lee Stuart; Art Buyer: Christine Saunders;
Concept Illustrator: David Bray; Designer: Mary Lam

'The great thing about advertising is it's part idea, part technology,
and 100% mystery.' John Hegarty

Photographer: David Stewart; Art Director: Ed Morris; Copywriter: Ed Morris; Art Buyer: Gary Wallis; Agency: Lowe; Client: Nestle (Quality Street)

'The Quality Street ads have a real honesty and humour – they didn't try to get a lovely blue morning when the train had stopped!' John Hegarty

MANIC STREET PREACHERS LIFEBLOOD

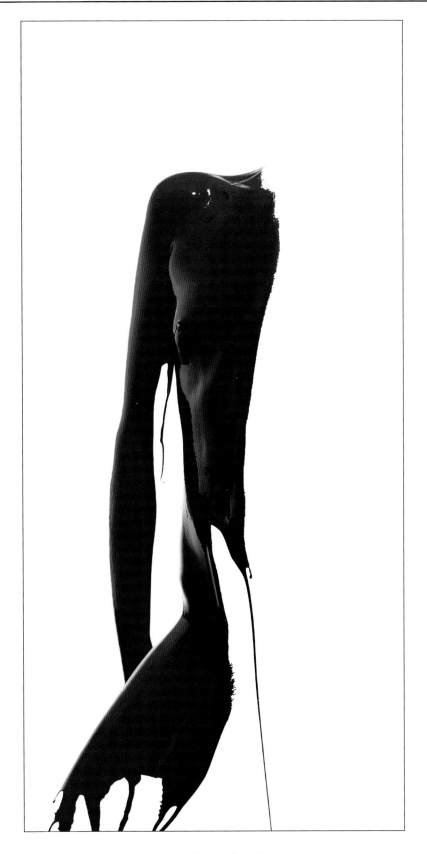

'I think that this is absolutely fantastic – many people have mentioned it.' Mike Denny

'The sheer imagination and freshness of depicting a shape and form – that is what photography is all about.'
John Hegarty

'It's also the simplicity of it, you engage with it.'
Samantha Thomas

Design and direction: Farrow Design; Photography: John Ross;
Image manipulation: Metro Imaging

'It works because it takes you to a point – and great ideas make you jump just a little bit further – in other words they engage with your imagination. This is a brilliant example of making my imagination work that little bit harder and therefore I reward the design, the photography and everyone comes away winning.'

John Hegarty

Design and direction: Farrow Design; Photography: John Ross;
Image manipulation: Metro Imaging

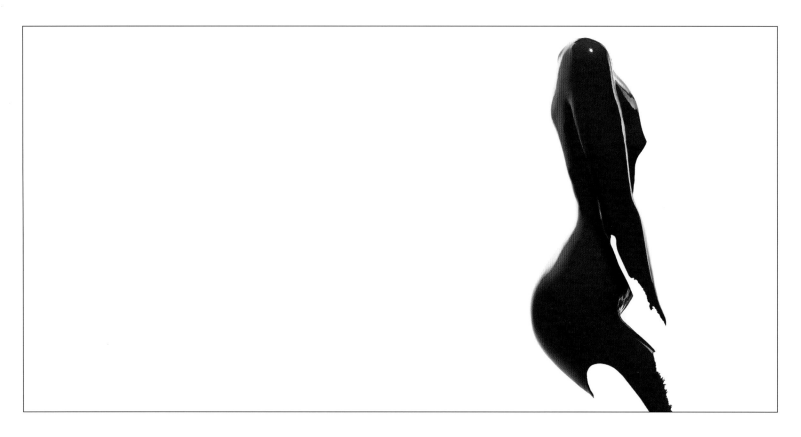

Design and direction: Farrow Design; Photography: John Ross;
Image manipulation: Metro Imaging

**'Depicting lifeblood is
just so well handled,
so beautifully done.'** Mike Denny

future
face

image
identity
innovation
sandra
kemp

Client: Sandra Kemp; Author: RCA and The Wellcome Trust; Designer: Morag Myerscough, Studio Myerscough;
Photographer: Michael Najjar; Title: dana_2.0

'This book cover perfectly captures the contents' debate about
where we are going and what we are going to look like and why. It is
summed up by this picture.' Mike Denny

Client: Conran Shop; Designer: Morag Myerscough, Studio Myerscough;
Art Directors: Morag Myerscough, Studio Myerscough and Polly Dickens, Conran Shop; Photographer: Richard Learoyd

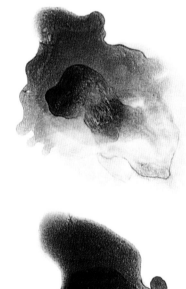

'Creating texture with photography and communicating it is a strong theme right now, and this is a delightful example.' Mike Denny

Client: Conran Shop; Designer: Morag Myerscough, Studio Myerscough;
Art Directors: Morag Myerscough; Photographer: Richard Learoyd; Retoucher: Robin Naish

'This is about using photography rather than the image itself.
It's about making colour work and unashamedly making it about
Christmas. It's all in the communication.' Samantha Thomas

Photographer: John Stillwell, Press Association

'If you had shown this picture five years ago you would have said: 'What on earth are these people doing, holding up their mobile phones in front of the Queen?' But today it's completely normal. John Hegarty

'Issue wise and photography wise, the pictures speak for themselves – the whole climate of fear, the use of children – all communicated through these images, and in a mainstream magazine.' Samantha Thomas

Editor: Eric Pooley; Picture Editors: Mike Bealing and Julius Domoney; Design: Paul Lussier and Yvonne McCrimon

Photographer: Yuri Kozyrev / For Time

Photographer: Kuri Kochetcov / EPA

GOODBYE: Relatives mourn two sisters killed at the school

MORTUARY: The bodies of the dead fill the Beslan schoolyard

WASTELAND: Locals survey the wrecked school gymnasium

FINISHED: One of the insurgents lies dead in a classroom

CLEANUP: Emergency workers sift through debris at the school

THE SCHOOL SIEGE

CHECHEN HOSTAGE CRISES: A HISTORY
Seizing captives is a favored rebel tactic

JUNE 1995 Seven months into the first phase of the Chechen war, separatists take 1,600 hostages at a hospital in Budennovsk, in southern Russia. They demand that Moscow stop the fighting and hold talks with rebel President Jokhar Dudayev. During a weeklong siege 120 die, many in failed Russian attempts to take the building. The hostages are released after the fighters are given free passage to Chechnya in a convoy, using 150 people as human shields.

JANUARY 1996 Chechen fighters take 2,000 hostages at another hospital, this one in Kizlyar in Dagestan. Some 300 rebels move back toward Chechnya, again using hostages as human shields. As Russian forces engage them in an unsuccessful rescue attempt in the village of Pervomayskaya, 78 hostages die. Meanwhile, in an attempt to draw attention to the Chechen cause, nine pro-Chechen Turks seize control of a passenger ferry docked in the Turkish Black Sea port of Trabzon, holding the 242 passengers and crew captive. All the hostages are released when the hijackers surrender to police.

OCTOBER 2002 Chechen insurgents led by Movsar Barayev take control of Moscow's Theater Center on Dubrovka, holding more than 800 people hostage. Women with explosive belts strapped to their waists take part in the raid. After a four-day standoff, Russian special forces storm the building after flooding the theater with an aerosol version of a powerful painkiller, Fentanyl. All 41 guerrillas are killed; 129 hostages also die, many as a result of the Fentanyl derivative.

> **ONE PUSH AND THE CAUCASUS WILL BE ENGULFED IN ONE BLOODY, SENSELESS MELEE.** —RUSLAN KHASBULATOV, former Duma Speaker

TIME, SEPTEMBER 13, 2004

Photographer (left): Vladamir Svartsevich / Argumenty & Fakty Weekly For Time

Photographer (right): Photoprom For Time

WE MADE IT: A mother and daughter comfort one another after surviving the siege

ANGUISH: Terrified and dehydrated, these boys managed to escape from the school

"You animals! You sheep! Why won't you shut up," one of the fighters yelled. They pulled a male hostage up so everyone could see him. "If you don't shut up, we'll kill him. After that we will kill a woman, then a child."

Regional officials started talking to the gunmen, and Russian diplomats arranged for a late-night Security Council meeting calling for the hostages' immediate freedom. But from inside School No. 1, the terrorists made their own demands: the withdrawal of Russian troops from Chechnya and the release of their comrades imprisoned in Ingushetia. Russian officials ordered broadcasters not to repeat the demands, and an offer by Chechen separatist leader Aslan Maskhadov to go to the scene to negotiate the hostages' safe return, contingent upon guarantees of his own safety, was also suppressed. The terrorists rejected offers of safe passage and suggestions of swapping children for adult hostages, and even turned down offers of food and water—fearing that supplies could be drugged, or that their delivery could provide cover for an attack.

Relatives waiting at the Palace of Culture were growing restless and angry at the lack of news. On the second day, a senior Interior Ministry official and the press secretary of President Dzasokhov showed up to give them a rundown of events. One repeated the official line that there were 354 hostages, which the relatives knew was bunk. "Have you no shame?" a woman shouted. "How can we trust you if you can't even count the number of hostages?" yelled a man. The officials quickly left.

Inside the gymnasium, there was one positive sign. Ruslan Aushev, an Afghan war hero and former President of Ingushetia, went into the school to negotiate. Bitterly disliked by the Kremlin, he is widely respected in the Caucasus because he rejects terrorism but is sympathetic to the Chechen cause. Before he entered the gym, the rebels put on their masks and told the hostages to lie still. Aushev entered the room and surveyed the hellish scene. "I understand," Kasumova heard him say. "There will be negotiations." The masked men agreed to release mothers with babies; 26 people reached safety. But the hostages' relatives milling around the town's Palace of Culture, desperate for news, could still hear sporadic gunfire and explosions coming from the school.

Inside the gym on Friday morning, a rumor passed from hostage to hostage that they would soon be released. Kasumova didn't know where it came from or whether to believe it. But the guerrillas seemed to be waiting for something, too. A deal had been struck for members of the search-and-rescue service to remove some corpses. Dressed in blue overalls with bright red stripes, with the logo and initials of the service prominently displayed on their backs, six officers approached the entrance to the gym at about 1:05 p.m. The men weren't wearing bulletproof vests or carrying guns. That's when the great explosion ripped the air, and the final battle began. Two of the search-and-rescue officers were gunned down by rebels.

It still isn't clear what triggered the explosion, whether it was intentional or a mishap. Russian officials say it was a rebel booby trap. The security forces appeared unprepared for the chaos, implying that the government had not abandoned its commitment to negotiate, but that something had gone awry. "This melee seems to have come up quite unexpectedly and went out of control," said one special-forces officer in Moscow. But some journalists on the scene thought the apparent disorganization could have been cover for an attack that had been planned all along, citing as evidence the deployment of crack troops, tanks and special forces the night before, and the imposition of reporting restrictions that often precede major raids.

NO MATTER WHO INITIATED THE FINAL battle, the deadly result was a crushing defeat for the security forces and for Putin, who has carefully constructed an image as the man whose uncompromising toughness can deliver security to Russians. The bloodbath, with chaotic scenes of half-naked, bloody children running through the streets, cruelly mocked those promises.

Analysts stressed the danger of a spiral of reprisals between the largely Christian Ossetians, outraged at the school carnage, and the predominantly Muslim Ingush, some of whom were said to be among the hostage takers. Only hours after the siege ended, the reprisals seemed to have begun. According to human-rights activist Timur Aliyev, who was in Beslan during the siege, Ossetians took a handful of Ingush hostages in the village of Chermen, 20 km southeast of the grieving town. "Tensions are mounting," Aliyev says.

That's bad news for Putin and for the whole of the Caucasus. In 1992, North Ossetia and Ingushetia fought briefly but violently over the disputed district of Prigorodny in North Ossetia. About 1,000 people died, and between 40,000 and 60,000 Ingush were forced out of Prigorodny before Russian troops intervened. The conflict has been smoldering ever since. "One push, like a new Ossetian-Ingush war, and the entire Caucasus will be engulfed in one bloody, senseless and hopeless melee that Russia will not have enough troops to contain," says Ruslan Khasbulatov, former Speaker of the Russian parliament.

Putin wasted no time declaring he would crack down even harder rather than negotiate a political solution to the Chechen conflict. In his televised speech on Saturday, he paraphrased Stalin: "We have shown weakness. The weak ones get beaten." With the Kremlin claiming that nine of the terrorists in Beslan were of Arab descent—something independent observers have not yet been able to confirm—Putin blamed the crisis on the "direct intervention of international terrorism" aimed at breaking up Russia. He promised a new "set of measures to reinforce the country's unity," as well as tougher rule in the Caucasus and a new "crisis management system" that would enhance the powers of the security services. Some observers, including senior officers in the security services, worried that these new measures could be used to further enhance Putin's power, entrenching the country ever deeper in his authoritarian rule.

The Chechen conflict doesn't fit easily into the "war on terror." Most Chechens do not share al-Qaeda's religious fundamentalism, and they don't seek a return of the caliphate. What they want is their own state, something Putin has vowed never to give them. But Chechen rebels and foreign Islamic terrorists do have links that have grown stronger as the war for independence has dragged on.

Arab militants have been apprehended in Georgia's Pankisi Gorge, a former haven for Chechen separatists, and a fundamentalist wing of the Chechen resistance has been gaining influence inside Chechnya. The hard-line guerrilla leader Shamil Basayev, the man alleged to have masterminded the Moscow theater siege, receives money from Middle Eastern and Gulf states, and has produced fund-raising videos with Arabic voice-overs. And the Islambouli Brigades, a little-known group that claims al-Qaeda links, says it brought down the two Russian airliners two weeks ago in revenge against Russian policies in Chechnya—but there is no known connection between the Islambouli Brigades and Chechen separatists.

> **OUTSIDE THE SCHOOL, THE GUERRILLAS OPENED FIRE ON US, AND I SAW ONE CHILD GO DOWN, AND THEN ANOTHER.** —ELENA KASUMOVA, teacher at School No. 1

TIME, SEPTEMBER 13, 2004

TIME, SEPTEMBER 13, 2004

Photographer: Musa Sadulayev / AP

Photographer: EPA / Stringer

IN SAFE HANDS: A man rushes a wounded girl away from the school

Photographer: Dmitry Khrutov

Photographer: Dmitry Khrutov / Novye Izvestia — EPA

Photographer: Yuri Kozyrev / For Time

WRENCHING REUNION: Families find their murdered loved ones at a nearby morgue

SHELTER: Soldiers and civilians take cover on a special forces storm the school building

E SHOWN WEAKNESS. THE WEAK GET BEATEN. "
—VLADIMIR PUTIN, Russian President

TIME, SEPTEMBER 13 2004

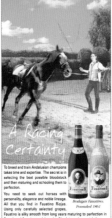

'This is a case of perfectly summing up a person, a place and a time. A leader who came and went quietly.' Mike Denny

Photographer: Jonathan Evans, Independent Newspaper

THE INDEPENDENT
Thursday 16 September 2004

HUNTING PROTESTS

3

the hunting lobby were in full cry

'A gentleman in his uniform with blood on his face. Perfectly displaying the conflict of the time.' John Hegarty

Police used truncheons to beat back protesters, as MPs sought to force through a ban

How protest by tweed and flat-cap brigade descended into pitched battle with police

IT BEGAN as a peaceful demonstration by civilised people concerned that a part of the British way of life was under threat. But yesterday's protest by the Countryside Alliance at the bill to ban hunting was marred by violence, ugly scenes of confrontation and one of the biggest breaches of security in the Houses of Parliament.

The atmosphere in Parliament Square had been calm as people from all over the country gathered to protest at the Government's attempt to force the bill through in one day. The sound of hunting horns and whistles coupled with a preponderance of tweed jackets and flat caps created a very different

BY TERRY KIRBY
AND HELEN McCORMACK

atmosphere in an area normally dominated by tourists and civil servants.

But this protest was not a simple show of defiance, it was a desperate attempt to derail an unstoppable legislative train.

Graeme and Georgie Worsley, joint masters of a the Old Surrey, Burstow and West Kent Hunt, had come straight from a morning's hunting, with their two children, Hector 10 and Tabitha, 9. Mr Worsley, 39, a landscape manager, said: 'This is being steamrolled through the House of Commons with little evidence that it really represents the wishes of the

majority of British people."

By mid-afternoon, the crowd had swelled to 20,000, and egged on by platform speakers, the mood became more militant.

At about 3.30pm a series of scuffles broke out in the south-west corner of the Square as a small number of protesters attempted to break through the police lines. They set off smoke bombs and lobbed plastic bottles and placards at police officers. Protesters claimed that the scuffles had been provoked by the police calling them "losers".

Although platform speakers appealed for calm the militants were urged on by some of the crowd.

Quin Hough, of Lincolnshire, a Countryside

Alliance steward, said: "We did not want this sort of mayhem. We are not fighting the police. They have their job to do and we have our protest."

On the other side of the Square, another group of demonstrators staged a sit-down protest, blocking the road across Westminster Bridge. Police were eventually forced to carry many protesters away.

Scotland Yard said 11 people had been arrested for offences including breach of the peace, disorderly behaviour and using threatening words and behaviour. Nineteen people are thought to have been injured of which 17 were members of the public and two were police officers.

Photographer: Jonathan Evans, Independent Newspaper

'The picture should be an interative document of our time.' Samantha Thomas

Photographer: Timothy Allen, Independent Newspaper

HO/AFP/Getty Images

Jeff Haynes/AFP/Getty Images   'You think of a moment – and you think
of that picture.' Mike Denny

10 | G2 in China Arts 09.11.04 | 11

Is Chinese art kicking butt… or kissing it?

Collectors are queueing up to buy work by China's bright young artists. But while the scene is certainly buzzing, some worry that the domestic art world is selling out to the west, says **Charlotte Higgins**

A t 50 Moganshan Street in Shanghai is a clump of dusty warehouses and small-scale factories, hedged around by a tall, encroaching thicket of tower blocks. Inside the compound can be glimpsed the busy activity of small-scale industry. A door lies ajar to reveal a dingy shoebox of a room, closely packed with bunk beds to accommodate migrant workers.

The building next door, by contrast, fronts the world with a sparkling plate-glass window; behind it is a minimalist office interior, Mies van der Rohe chairs set at neat angles. For 50 Moganshan Street is where, alongside the low-rent workshops, Shanghai's high-end contemporary art world has come to roost. Round every corner you'll find an artist's studio, or an exclusive dealer selling Chinese art for thousands of dollars out of some glamorously dilapidated warehouse. It's like a wet dream of SoHo in the early days.

People talk of an "explosion" of Chinese art. For a country that has virtually no contemporary art history, where artists' training is dominated by an ultra-traditional grounding in Chinese painting techniques, where the first clues as to what was happening in the post-modern western art world trickled through as recently as the late 1980s, the scene has mushroomed and transmuted with staggering velocity, artists running through mini-movements (political pop art, the much discussed trend for body art in the mid-1990s, through to a strong focus today on installation, film and video) with alarming speed. In Europe and the US, Chinese art is, as they say, hot. Of the art sold at Moganshan Street, the vast majority is to collectors from abroad. "Kissing foreigners' arses" is how one young art graduate dismissively describes it.

"China keeps being discovered," says Davide Quadrio, a touch wearily. An Italian long-term resident of the city, he is a curator who, for the past five years, has run a not-for-profit art centre, his current space accessible via a juddering goods lift up in a Moganshan Street warehouse.

"Chinese art is overexposed to foreign journalists, curators, dealers. And for some young artists it's difficult to deal with the expectations. People seem to have an overwhelming need for China at the moment – ideas from China, novelty from China. But you can't find 10 or 15 new young artists each year."

Quadrio has been one of the chief actors in the drama that has seen artistic activity in Shanghai transmute over the past decade "from an era of guerrillas to the era of a regular army", as artist Qiu Zhijie has put it. He recalls how, from a low-profile underground, with artists showing avant-garde work mainly to each other in their studios, a more public scene took shape. In 1996, Lorenz Hebling, a Swiss art dealer, set up the first private commercial gallery focused purely on contemporary Chinese work. A turning point came in 1999, when Quadrio's outfit, Bizart, put on an exhibition called Art For Sale. It was Shanghai's first large-scale show of avant-garde art outside the nascent commercial gallery circuit. "It was closed down after two days for pornography," says Quadrio, "but it was illegal anyway – we we had squatted a mall." Despite its short life and a furious denunciation in the press, it was a huge success, ambitious in scale and intent, a call to arms for Shanghai artists.

Quadrio was now determined to set up a permanent, not-for-profit exhibition space. It wasn't as easy as it might sound. A cultural organisation in the city has no legal status unless affiliated to the government, thus coming under the power of the Shanghai Cultural Bureau. Such control, from a conservative, bureaucratic and extremely circumspect body, was never going to be viable for Quadrio. The way round it was to create a wholly owned Chinese company, becoming a "commercial enterprise in the eyes of the Chinese authorities". The numerous events and exhibitions he has held since then fly, mostly, below the radar of officialdom. It is one of many subtle accommodations Quadrio has come to with the authorities. "You play with the limits, and the government lets you play," he says. Money, rather than censorship, he stresses, is the biggest headache: Quadrio hires out his curatorial and technical skills to help pay for the programme, and works with foreign funders and foundations, including Arts Council England.

In one neighbouring warehouse, Li Liang, an artist and dealer, runs a gallery called Eastlink. He is an urbane, sleek figure, his office cluttered with artworks: 2ft-long rat sculptures by Jin Le, vulgarly entertaining multicoloured resin figures by Li Zhan Yang. "I'm doing two things," he says. "I have to have something to sell. And then there are exhibitions. **page 12 ▶**

Body of work… digital photographic work by Liu Wei

China fact
61m
The number of Chinese investors in the stock market. There are 60m members of the Chinese Communist Party

Photographers: Dan Chung and Don McPhee; Picture Editor: Sarah Gilbert; Layout: Rick Williams

'The Chinese are going to have some problems, with the new challenges that they are to face as a free society. This is what this image tells us.' John Hegarty

>**Moments
In the Pink**
Reiner Riedler

When times are tough, a girl puts her best
dress on, holds her head high and gets
on her horse. The Russian State Circus,
once a prestigious cultural ambassador
of the Soviet Union, was hardly able to
feed its animals as the red star of
communism faded. Many performers
left Russia to live in the west. Artistic
reputations were ruined as disreputable
showmen used famous names to lure
audiences.

A new generation of circus directors, like
Mstislav Zapashny, of Rosgostsirk, are
reversing this trend by catching up with
slick circus entertainment and enticing
the performing elite back home.

The fallen state is back in her saddle. 8

Photographer: Reiner Riedler; Editor: Jon Levy; Design: Rob & Phil; Published by foto8 (www.foto8.com)

Home to Roost
Mary-Jane Maybury

There are nearly three quarters of a million empty homes in England, 100,000 of which are in London. Some were repossessed, when people could no longer pay the mortgage or couldn't pay the rent and were evicted. Others await clearance after the death of the occupant. There are a multitude of reasons why people move on, often they don't have a choice. This bird shit-encrusted sofa was one of the things that got left behind **8**

Photographer: Mary-Jane Maybury; Editor: Jon Levy; Design: Rob & Phil; Published by foto8 (www.foto8.com)

O! Say
Can
You See ...

12

Photographer: Christopher Morris; Editor: Jon Levy; Design: Rob & Phil; Published by foto8 (www.foto8.com)

Christopher Morris "In the Name of God the Flag and Bush Almighty". This is my America, my New Republic. If the hijackers on September 11 accomplished anything, this is it. They have given us the divine Bush. A man who has said "you are either with us or against us". A man who teaches our children that "they hate us because we love freedom".

This is my America. An America with a Homeland Security, a Patriot Act. An America with paranoia. An America with hatred and ignorance. An America that wraps itself in its President and its flag. This is my America.

Now when I see the eagle of freedom, I see an eagle of fascism. Now when I see the American flag, I'm afraid. I'm afraid for my America. We have become an ugly nation. A nation that has wrapped its eyes so tightly in red, white and blue that it is blind. Blinded by nationalism. This is my America. And this is why they hate us, and its not because we love freedom. They hate us because we think like that **8**

13

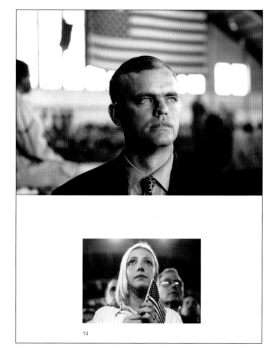

14

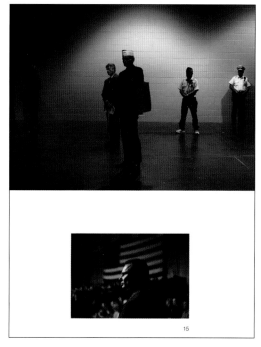

15

16

17

18

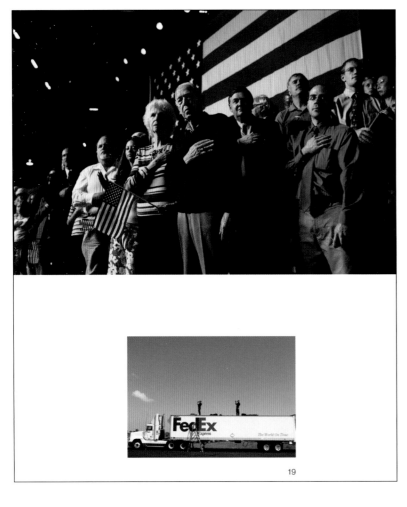

20

19

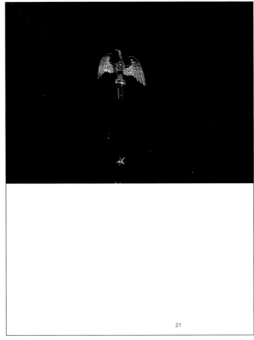

21

Photographer: Sean Smith; Picture Editor: Sarah Gilbert; Designer: Roger Browning

2 | Travels with the Territorials

14.10.04 | 3

They are bankers, abattoir workers, solicitors and HGV drivers, but they also have a second job – part-time soldiers. Foreign correspondent of the year **Audrey Gillan** was given unique access to the Territorial Army in southern Iraq, where she found out what it's like to be fixing the office photocopier one day – and getting shot at the next. Photographs by **Sean Smith**

The weekend warriors go to war

The shots are not quite as loud as you might expect them to be, but still they are too close for comfort. The bullets fly past the head of a shocked Territorial Army soldier and embed themselves in the wall, just inches from where he is standing. A sharp voice shouts: "Contact to our left, three or four rounds." Seconds later, there is a small burst of fire.

They call it a contact and what it means is that somebody, somewhere, shot at British troops. It happens every single day in Iraq. Today they think it might be a warning that they have stayed in this area for too long, but in truth they really don't know. It is one of the first forays British soldiers have made into the town of Amara, north of Basra, for quite a while and the locals aren't happy. On the wall of a nearby community centre, a scrawl in red paint reads: "Dawn No No USA British [sic]".

This group of 12 Territorial Army soldiers from 52 Lowland Regiment Y Company have been escorting a man from the Ministry of Defence to another British-built community centre. The civil servant – known as a political adviser, or "polad" for short – has flown up from Basra to check that British government funds are being properly spent. Colour Sergeant Keith Irving from Hawick in the Scottish Borders is in charge of this expedition, and is standing on a street outside the community centre, watching for possible trouble, his SA80 rifle at the ready. He is surrounded by dozens of cheeky **page 4 ▶**

'The picture should be an interative document of our time... and how it is presented is the facilitation of that communication.' Samantha Thomas

4 | Travels with the Territorials

14.10.04 | 5

◂ page 3 faced children shouting, "Mister, mister, Saddam donkey," while showing him the soles of their feet. But as the convoy pulls off later, the children's faces turn resentful and they start throwing stones.

It's just another day for the Territorial Army soldiers serving in Iraq – people who, most of the time, live daily lives every bit as ordinary and banal as yours or mine, but who find themselves, in times of war, called upon to do an extraordinary second job in a very dangerous place. The mobilisation of reservists for the war in Iraq was the biggest since the Suez Crisis, and it continues to grow through the postwar phase. There are 1,210 Territorial Army soldiers serving on Op Telic 4, as the current operation in Iraq is known, making up 14% of the 8,069-strong British force. Roughly 10% of the TA contingent are female, many of them nurses.

As the British army has come to rely ever more heavily on part-time soldiers, the contrast between the jobs they do at home and what they do in "theatre", as the military call the Iraqi conflict zone, has become more striking than ever. There is the Calor Gas tanker driver who is currently gathering intelligence; the joiner who runs a job creation scheme for Iraqi people; the marketing officer for the National Archive at Kew who now spends his days trying to liaise with public service officials; as well as the mechanics, plumbers and City analysts doing guard duty. Then there are those on a busman's holiday of sorts: the two electricity specialists working on the Basra power grid; the doctors and nurses working in the military field hospital; the chefs now preparing meals for thousands of soldiers stationed in the desert.

The soldiers from 52nd Lowland Regiment have spent most of their time in Iraq on force protection, interspersed with what they consider the more boring job – guard duty. They are coming to the end of their six-month stint in Amara and their morale is still pretty high. At home, they belong to various TA units, training in their different bases in Edinburgh, Glasgow, Ayr and other towns across Scotland during the week, coming together as a brigade at periodic short residential camps. While they may have met each other's wives and families at dances and other TA events, they don't like to talk about home too much.

Irving, the broad-accented Scotsman, is typical of the TA soldiers here in that he believes that he is just as professional as any regular in the field. He served in the regulars for five years, then signed up with the TA 10 years after leaving the forces. "Having seen it from both sides of the fence, I think commitment-wise the TA guy is the better soldier," he says. We are standing outside a British-funded blacksmith's shop. Inside, the owner is telling the MoD man that he is now employing five members of his family because of the funds he received to kit out his workshop. The MoD man is happy, even though this marks just a small success in terms of the British attempt to help rebuild the country.

Outside on the street there is a perception that the tension is mounting. The road is busy with cars and bicycles and people, all of them staring: most don't look particularly friendly. It's not the numbers on the street you need to worry about, says Irving, it's when the crowd suddenly disappears that you know something might go wrong. I ask him if he ever gets scared. He shrugs his shoulders and quips: "Wit's for ye will no go by ye," a fatalistic Scottish expression which means whatever happens happens. In his other life, Irving delivers medical oxygen across the Borders of Scotland.

***

Another day, another scene. It is just past 7am and a watery sun is burning a hazy white light across the flat landscape that British soldiers have taken to calling the "Gifa". Territorial army fusilier Michael Greville explains that it means the "great Iraqi fuck all".

Greville is 26, and usually works as a credit analyst for Cazenove, a city investment bank. It's an office-bound job and most days he finds himself by a computer. In Iraq, when he is not soldiering, he goes back to his accommodation to study his notes for the chartered financial analyst exam which he hopes to take next year: "When I am really bored, which is pretty much 12 hours a day when we are not working, I go back to my room and study." Being here means he is missing out on his city bonuses, but Greville is enjoying the tour anyway.

This morning some of Four Platoon from Messines Company, the London Regiment, are on their way north, escorting three vehicles from the British divisional headquarters at Basra airbase to the Dutch army camp near the town of Samawa, south of the flashpoint city of Najaf. Like 52 Lowland, they provide armed escort and covering fire should the convoy of regular troops meet any insurgency on the road.

They may work alongside the regulars, but ultimately all the TA soldiers in Iraq are under the command of the British Forces General Officer Commanding Major General Rollo, who is a regular soldier. Those serving with Messines Company are led by a TA Major Conrad Giles whilst those attached to a regular regiment such as the Princess of Wales's Royal Regiment take orders from a regular commanding officer. The TA frequently provides protection for regular soldiers who are not fighting on the frontline but who have to move around southern Iraq. In such situations the regular soldier must obey the TA unit's senior ranking soldier.

In this instance it is Colour Sergeant Rob Denman, and he is calling out orders through the radio to the two guys in each of the vehicles whose heads are sticking out through a hole in the roof to provide covering fire. They are known as "top cover" and find themselves in one of the most exposed situations of all the military – a number of the recent deaths and injuries in Iraq amongst British troops were of soldiers doing top cover.

Up top, one soldier faces the front and another the back, one with an SA80, one with a Minimi light machine gun, both looking for a possible threat. They cautiously keep their eyes open for snipers, mortar teams, rocket propelled grenades (RPGs) and the particularly lethal improvised explosive devices, IEDs, that can be left on the side of the road and detonated some distance away by remote control. If the convoy stops or slows for too long, they must dismount and try to move the traffic on while at the same time watching out for potential assaults. The rebels in the south have yet to use the suicide car bombs seen in Baghdad, but the soldiers are anxious that they soon could.

"Just so you are aware, there's one pax [person] standing up on that flatbed coming towards us," says Denman. "As we move up the MSR [main supply route] make sure the vehicles are tight. I don't want no civvies in between us." The previous night, another Messines Company force protection team was the target of an RPG, which shot through the gap between two of their vehicles. They need to stay close.

Nicknamed the Colourman because of his rank, Denman is 37 and works as a principal officer at Wandsworth prison. An hour and a half outside of Basra, he spots a cloud of black smoke up ahead. He tells the boys to approach slowly. They soon realise it's a traffic accident involving a Dutch military vehicle and a local car.

Three Iraqis have died in the accident (the casualties were quickly removed by locals), but the Dutch soldiers have been standing by the side of the road for a while apparently doing nothing to police the situation. "Maybe they are in shock," says Denman. He jumps down from his wagon and orders his soldiers to enact the drill they have trained for to deal with this situation. Denman starts to set up a vehicle checkpoint and control the traffic; the rest of the guys are sent to guard the peripheral area. An hour and a half later, the Dutch "quick reaction force" arrives and he can

"You took the slagging that you were Saturday and Sunday troops, but how can your friends turn around and say that now?

When I am really bored, which is pretty much 12 hours a day, I go back to my room and study

Regular soldiers take six weeks to do a course that takes us two weeks because they're not as brainy as us

We do use live rounds sometimes when we are training in the UK, but there's a different apprehension about it here

I'm paid by society to carry out a task, I am paid to be a soldier and follow the orders of my commanding officer

They shoot first, it's them or us. I'd rather go home and see my two kids"

stand his men down. "It's not very quick, the quick reaction force, is it?" someone pipes up. "Yesh, we have just come from Camp Shpliffy," cracks another. The Dutch, whose camp is called Smitty, are the butt of a lot of British jokes.

Denman calls his boys "the PlayStation generation" because "all they can use is their thumbs" but really, he admits, "I think they are the mutts nuts because they bring all their outside experience to the job – and today they showed that the TA can do the same job as the regular army."

In the team – as well as the prison officer, the nurse, and the City boy – are: Lance Corporal Ander Broadman, 30, who procures engineering works for Network Rail and missed out on a vital promotion by being in Iraq; private Ed Elliott, nicknamed Billy (as in Billy Elliott), who works for JP Morgan Fleming in the city and "likes this sort of stuff, it's a break from delays on the Northern Line and fixing the photocopier"; Private Tom Kelly, nicknamed Forceps because of the shape of his skull, who drives a HGV lorry for the Post Office; Dean "Deano" Moore, a shaven-headed joker of a joiner from Belfast and Private Tim "Watesy" Wates, a recently redundant recruitment consultant who joined the TA "to shoot stuff. Not people, but to shoot off weapons, the feel, the sound, the power there's a huge adrenalin rush: it's boys' toys".

Pace, who could have been a medic in the TA but preferred to join the infantry, says: "It's like training for a football match and wanting to play. I didn't want to train and just use blanks in a forest somewhere. We do use live rounds when we are training sometimes in the UK but there's a different apprehension about it." Wates pipes in: "That's what gives it the edge, you know there are people out there wanting to kill you."

***

Britain has a long history of reserve forces, with Volunteer and Yeomanry units being formed during the Napoleonic wars. The TA was established in 1907. First known as the Territorial Force, it encouraged Britons to join in "homeland defence": the word territorial signified that those who served with the force were under no obligation to serve overseas. By 1921 it had changed its name to the Territorial Army. In the first world war, a number TA units volunteered to go to war and did not come back for four years, bringing back 71 Victoria Crosses for bravery.

With the abolition of national service and the advent of the cold war, it seemed the TA's role was assured, but with the fall of the iron curtain, the security of the homeland was deemed to be under rather less of a threat. The Conservatives cut TA numbers by 15,000 between 1991 and 1994, then the present government scythed the numbers further from 54,000 to 41,000 as part of the 1998 Strategic Defence Review. The then defence secretary George Robertson said: "The TA should no longer be a force of last resort, held against a major conventional threat to the UK and Nato allies. More units will be placed at significantly higher states of readiness. And we will now be prepared to call them up – in formed units if needs be – in situations that fall short of a direct threat to the UK such as the Gulf war." This would, he added, give them a "more heavy weight role". The 40,000-strong TA now forms 25% of the British army, and can be called on to provide the army with entire formed units or to supply individual specialists as required in IT, logistics, medicine, communications and other areas.

Almost all of them, while essentially volunteers, have been compulsorily mobilised (the MoD calls it "intelligent mobilisation", insisting that it accommodates people who can prove it would be impossible for them to go for professional or personal reasons). The Reserve Forces Act 1996 obliges all employers to keep a TA soldier's job open but some have returned from Iraq to find this isn't the case. At least page 7

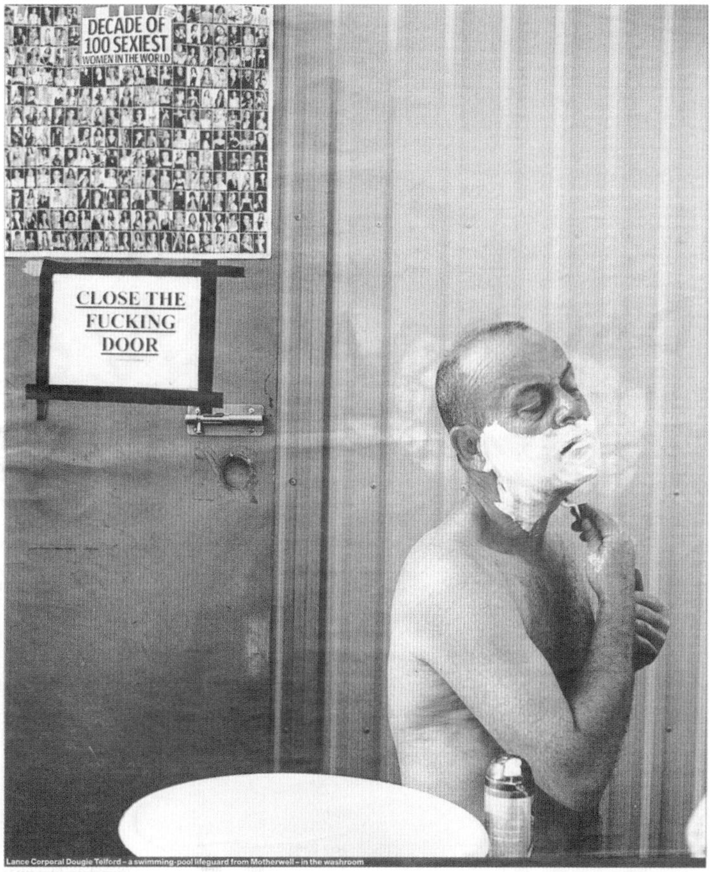

Lance Corporal Dougie Telford – a swimming-pool lifeguard from Motherwell – in the washroom

Photographer: Sean Smith; Picture Editor: Sarah Gilbert; Designer: Roger Browning

Graffiti greets TA soldiers on patrol in the town of Amara, north of Basra

◄ page 4 17 are believed to be taking their former employers to tribunals after losing their jobs upon their return.

Compared to the training undergone by regular soldiers, the territorials' induction can seem light. Soldiers attend training on three evenings each month, and commit themselves to one Sunday a month, and six weekends and two full weeks camp a year, which they must take out of their annual work leave. For these hours they are paid the same as a regular soldier of equivalent rank, ranging from £39.10 a day for a private to £102.51 for a major. Each year they are awarded a tax-free bounty of between £350 and £1,380 depending on length of service and on passing an annual battlefield weapons and fitness test. While they are mobilised, their salaries from their employers are suspended. The theory goes that a TA soldier on active service will be no worse off than he or she would be at home but sometimes this doesn't work out: a City trader can't expect to get his or her bonuses, but will get their mortgage and other "reasonable" outgoings covered.

Inevitably, the "Terries" take a ribbing from both civilians and the regular army for "playing" at being soldiers, a dads' army of weekend warriors. The comedian Jack Dee recently described members of the TA as "part-time soldier, full-time banging on about it", while the best-known fictional TA member, Gareth from the Office, never lets his own service go forgotten: "A lot of people think that the Territorial Army are not real soldiers. We are. We are well trained, highly disciplined fighting machines ready for war. We're just not available during the week."

"Until the TA changes their courses to six weeks like the regular army we will never be seen as them," says one soldier from 52nd Lowland. "But it takes them six weeks to do a course that takes us two weeks because they are not as brainy as us. That's why when regular guys leave the army the best job they can get is as a security adviser. But TA guys are different." In addition, the concept of rank can work rather differently with the territorials. Often, highly qualified civilians prefer to remain privates in what they see as a break from responsibility. Better educated, white-collar professionals often find themselves taking orders from someone who comes from a blue-collar background.

Certainly there can be a marked difference in culture between regular and territorial units. Last year, I was embedded with a squadron of regular soldiers during the invasion of Iraq. Spending time with the TA in a similar situation, it seemed to me that the diversity and breadth of experience that these men and women had gained in their normal daily lives gave them more interesting things to talk about than their regular counterparts – and a rather different view of their involvement in the conflict. Most had signed up for the TA out of a sense of patriotism and duty, but they are far from army machines; as one, who had copies of The Spanish Civil War and The Rise and Fall of the British Empire by his bed, told me: "I am a historian and I suppose I am in love with the romanticism of it all." Another did not believe the war was justified but enjoyed the adventure of it.

Denman has been in the TA for 14 years – "promoted and demoted a couple of times" – and got his call-up papers for Iraq in January 2004. It was a blow to his wife Sandy and his two children, Amy, 11, and James, 7, but he has worked every other weekend as a prison officer so he is used to missing key family moments. He has gone on exercise to Estonia, Germany, Cyprus and Romania, but Iraq is his first proper tour of duty. With a few qualms, he says, he would be happy to come back for another. "It's given me an outlet physically, getting out and not being surrounded by walls, a feeling of not being hemmed in. **page 8 ▶**

Photographer: Sean Smith; Picture Editor: Sarah Gilbert; Designer: Roger Browning

◄ page 7   Like other soldiers, Denman has his own opinion about the war, but out here considers it irrelevant. "I look at it the same way I do in the prison service: I am paid by society to carry out a task. I am paid to be a prison officer and to lawfully detain people and out here I am paid to be a soldier and follow the orders of my commanding officer and carry out foreign policy."

His worst day in Iraq, he says, was when he went to the field hospital at Shaiba Logistics Base and saw a 22-year-old private from his company being fed through a straw. He had received a shrapnel wound in his throat when an IED exploded under his vehicle. "Because I am a platoon sergeant I feel really, really responsible," says Denman. "In a way you are a father figure; I feel responsible for my blokes. When you have been through all the training and the camaraderie and you see someone you don't want to see hurt hurt it makes you angry."

***

This kind of attack has become more frequent in the British-controlled south since August, when Moqtada al-Sadr declared a holy war on British troops. It is now very rare to see British soldiers on the ground in their soft berets, a style of dress that was much trumpeted by the MoD in the days immediately after the war. The British claim they still have 90% of public consent, but it doesn't seem like that on the ground.

The battle group further north in Amara, for instance, has been under the most sustained attack of any British unit since the Korean war, with 881 mortar rounds being fired at them since April. It is estimated that the Princess of Wales's Royal Regiment has fired 30,000 rounds of ammunition, more than was used by all troops in the invasion phase last year. In August, the former family home of the governor of Maysan province used by the British as the headquarters of their civil and military cooperation unit (known as "Cimic House") came under siege; during one 10-day period, 428 mortars were fired at it. The 100 or so soldiers there – a high percentage of them TA – had to sit and battle it out.

Hanging out in the humid, malodorous tent that is their home in Abu Naji camp, five miles outside Amara city centre, some of Colour Sergeant Irving's "jocks" (as the infantry privates in the 52 Lowland are known) recall the three-week battle of Cimic House. One soldier filmed the engagement: the camera tracks red tracer fire as it thrashes across the sky towards the building and then back out in returning fire. The subtitles count the 595 mortars, 10% of which landed within the perimeter: 57 RPG attacks, five 107mm rocket attacks and 86 small arms engagements.

"I wouldn't say it was horrific," says Fusilier Derek Currie. "It was mad. A mortar knocked our sanger [an elevated guard post on the edge of camp] and deafened me for 8½ hours." Currie is 21 and from Glasgow. In his normal life he works with children in after-school care: "I do training, I do workshops with new employers, I organise sports days." Private David McCauley, 29, works in a call centre for the Manpower employment agency. "It's not scary at the time but you sit down after and go, oh God, that was a bit hairy."

But a boy with chipmunk teeth pipes up that it's "brilliant". Private Craig Hardie is 24 and a mechanic from Kelso, and he loves all this. He joined the TA 18 months ago, around the time of the fall of Saddam Hussein. Having trained in battlefield first aid he is the team medic, and the boys have stuck the label "witch doctor" above his camp bed. This kind of engagement, he says, is "what we join the TA for".

But however much it may seem to some like a great game, these boys, unlike many of the territorials in Iraq, have killed people. They know it should bother them, but at the time,

> ❝ I joined to shoot stuff. Not people, but shoot off weapons, the feel, the sound, the power. There's a huge adrenalin rush: it's boys' toys
>
> I have been nearby when a mortar has hit a civilian's house and the first thing I heard was a woman screaming, a sound you would never want to hear. I might not forget that
>
> Having seen it from both sides, I think commitment-wise the TA guy is the better soldier
>
> It's been the biggest waste of nine months of my life, because I have never done anything constructive to help the Iraqis
>
> If you slot someone, they are usually quite a distance away so, surprisingly, when you see them fall over it doesn't really affect you that much ❞

Rumours that the TA is hiring bring a large crowd of Iraqis to the Abu Naji camp

when the killing was done, it just didn't. "They shoot first: it's them or us," says McCauley. "I would rather go home and see my two kids. If you slot someone, they are usually quite a distance away, so surprisingly, when you see them fall over, it doesn't really affect you that much since they were firing at us first."

They say they are not worrying now about post-traumatic stress, or the many other psychological scars they may carry back to nine-to-five civilian lives. "Most of us here will be OK because we talk to each other about it," says McCauley. "I have been [nearby] when a mortar has hit a civilian's house and the first thing I have heard is a woman screaming, a sound you would never want to hear. I might not forget that."

Later, a regular soldier tells me a story about being at Cimic House. "I was on top of the Pink Palace with Keith [Irving] and we were crouched behind a really low parapet. I was shitting myself. I was on my belt buckle [lying down]. And Keith's up there with his rifle mounted over the parapet, bullets whizzing past him on either side and he's looking at me going: 'When your time's up you time's up.'" He adds admiringly: "And he's in the TA." Irving is not much of a stickler for ranks and titles. He and his sergeant Gordon Wylie, a plumber affectionately known as "Wee Speccy", believe that it is good for morale for the men to talk to each other like friends.

That night, at 1am, a loud bang, followed by a dull thud, shudders the ground on the eastern perimeter. Ten 107mm rockets – "a breast of a munition", says Irving – have landed and detonated. They are met by outgoing rounds from a Warrior tank. Just another contact, but this time the assault is much more sustained and it comes as a shock to TA Corporal Lisa Lovell, who is in the Royal Military Police. Sitting up in bed, a worried look on her face, she tells me that this is the most scared she has felt on her tour. She is a solicitor from Newcastle and thinks this fear may be because her time here is coming to an end. The soldiers believe that this is statistically the time when something bad might happen to them because they are apt to let their guard down.

***

Last month, the British moved out of Cimic House and handed it back to the Iraqis. Much of the work they were doing is now carried out from a cabin they call Cimic Hut that sits at the gates of Abu Naji; trips out of base are now very limited. On a table inside the hut, with the words "Compensation Claims" written on its spine, Sergeant William Cooper is looking at a photograph of a hole made in a wall by an RPG. A local woman, Jinan Salman Mohammed, hands over a photocopy of her identity card and a form which says, in English: "My house was bombed during the events between Al-Sadr militias and British forces by shelling by British army." In a box she details the damage and how much she reckons it will cost to build again. "Air conditioning, $400, blocks $250, sink and paint and glasses and basin with valves and mixer, $140, cement and sand, $300. Total: $1,340 US."

Cooper says it seems a pretty fair assessment – "sometimes, for damage to buildings they are trying for $10,000" – but says it is not clear who is to blame. "A lot of them bring these claims but they are not really sure who fired. We are trying to tell them that if we do fire any rockets or missiles it is all regulated and documented and we will know if it was us." In the past week they have had 30 claims for rocket damage.

Sitting beside him, Lance Corporal Dougie Telford, a swimming pool lifeguard from Motherwell, is looking at a set of photographs showing damage to a car and getting angry. "I saw this photograph yesterday with **page 10** ►

Each year, the AOP Student Photographer of the year receives a double page spread in the Awards book. Below are Emma Critchley's winning images from 2004.

AOP ASSISTANTS' AWARDS

LEFT TO RIGHT: DAMON COLLINS, KULBIR THANDI, JULIA FULLERTON-BATTEN

LEFT TO RIGHT: VALERIE HERSLEVEN, GRANT SMITH, NEIL SMITH

DAMON COLLINS Creative Director – Mother, began his career in 1986, at FCB. After moving to Gold Greenlees Trott to work under the legendary Dave Trott, he had spells at Leagas Shafron Davis Chick, as deputy Creative Director, Saatchi and Saatchi, as a creative Group Head and Abbott Mead Vickers, working for the other legendary Dave, or rather David. From there he moved to Lowe, where he was promoted to Creative Director. During his time there, the agency won awards on a wider range of brands than ever before, including Nestle and Unilever. He moved to Mother in early 2005. Over the years, Damon's work on accounts such as Yellow Pages, Anti-Smoking and Heineken has been recognised by numerous industry awards schemes.

JULIA FULLERTON-BATTEN is a photographer who is passionate about her work. In addition to shooting advertising campaigns and for editorial magazines, she always works on personal projects; many images are successful in international competitions. She has had her work accepted in the AOP Awards every year since 1998, including a series in this year's 2005 AOP Awards. She was also recognised this year for the Schweppes Awards, IPA Awards, PDN, Communication Arts and American Photography. Born in Germany, living several years in the USA, now settled in London, Julia has an international background and outlook. She is represented worldwide and shoots advertising campaigns globally.

VALERIE HERSLEVEN started her career as a photographer's agent in Belgium in 1997 with Special Bookings. In 1999 she centralised her photography business in London. Since 2003 she splits her time between Paris and London for her agency.

GRANT **S**MITH is an internationally acclaimed architectural and construction photographer. Australian born, he has resided in London since 1983 and his work includes many of the world's iconic structures: the Pont de Normandie, second Severn Crossing, the Sydney Harbour tunnel, the Millennium Bridge, the Millennium Dome and the Gherkin in London. He is represented in the National Portrait Gallery and is former Chairman of the Association of Photographers.

NEIL **S**MITH trained at Canterbury College of Art where he obtained a BA (hons) in Graphic Design. He then went on to work for Lloyd Northover before setting up GIANT in 1986. Between 1986 and 1997 GIANT's work was featured in the D&AD annual and won many design awards. In May 1997, Giant merged with Marsteller Advertising, the design practice of Burson Marsteller and Neil was appointed Design Director of Marsteller. Neil established his current design group, Howdy, in 1999. In his 25-year career, Neil has worked with many photographers for a wide range of clients including: Reuters, The Design Council, The British Council, The Labour Party, British Airways, Boots, Vauxhall Motors and the DTI.

KULBIR **T**HANDI started out photographing rocks for the Geological Survey in Leeds before moving to London to work as a black and white printer. He soon got a job as full-time assistant and within a few years he launched his own career. He now works on many prestigious advertising campaigns and is represented in both London and New York. He shoots mainly still life and more recently cars – though he has been known to shoot landscapes, people and food too.

Lifestyle & Portraiture SINGLE

DAN PRINCE   MERIT

PRINTER: Dan Prince

PHILIPPA COOPER

PRINTER: Philippa Cooper   TITLE: Shannon

PETER MALLET

TITLE: Josh

JOEL MICAH MILLER

PRINTER:
Joel Micah Miller

SYSTEM OPERATOR:
Henry Weber at Wild Voxel

DARREN PADGHAM
PRINTER: Mark Foxwell, Primary Colour

| ROB PAYNE

SAM ROBINSON

PRINTER: Michael Dyer Associates

JESSE STAGG

PRINTER: Jesse Stagg   Milford Sound, New Zealand

Lifestyle & Portraiture SERIES

PAUL THOMPSON

PRINTER: Lee Adams at Metro
SYSTEM OPERATOR:
John Swift and Paul Thompson

WINNER

THANKS TO: all sitters, David Stewart
and Rae Lyn at Metro

PEDRO ALVAREZ   MERIT
PRINTER: Pedro Alvarez

| MEIKE NIXDORF

Towergate Camerasure is now the largest provider of insurance solutions to the professional photographer market, and the recognised market leader, with strong links to the major trade associations within the industry. With over 20 years' experience, Towergate Camerasure offers a tailor-made insurance solution designed to meet the individual needs of both professional and amateur photographers/image makers.

Towergate Camerasure makes insurance easy to arrange by providing complete insurance cover under one simple and flexible policy. Part of the Towergate Underwriting Group one of the UK's leading specialist insurance groups, the policies are underwritten by Norwich Union, one of the largest insurance companies in the UK. This combination of strength and security gives you the reassurance of dealing with a name you can trust.

With friendly and knowledgeable staff, and a fast, efficient claims service, Towergate Camerasure provides insurance solutions you can trust, from a name you can rely on.

Fashion & Beauty SINGLE

LUISA VASQUES

PRINTER: Luisa Vasques

AOP ASSISTANTS' AWARDS

Fashion & Beauty SERIES

| ARMANDO FERRARI   WINNER

| MEIKE NIXDORF

COREL™

Corel UK is delighted to sponsor the AOP Assistants' Awards and we wish all final entrants, the industries most talented assistants, the very best of luck. Corel is renowned for its powerful software portfolio that combines innovative photo editing and graphics creation, vector-illustration and technical-graphics applications along with office and personal productivity solutions. Corel's flagship products include the CorelDRAW® Graphics Suite, Corel Painter Natural-Media® painting and illustration software and the Paint Shop™ Family of digital photography and image-editing software.

For more information on Corel products visit www.corel.co.uk

Landscapes, Interiors & Exteriors SINGLE

PEDRO ALVAREZ   WINNER
PRINTER: Pedro Alvarez

JESSE STAGG
PRINTER: Jesse Stagg

WINNER
Kaikoura, New Zealand

PEDRO ALVAREZ

PRINTER: Pedro Alvarez   Special thanks to Ernst

PEDRO ALVAREZ

PRINTER: Pedro Alvarez

Special thanks to Paul, Darren,
Julie and Barry

ROB PAYNE

SYSTEM OPERATOR:
Chris at Saddington Baynes

JESSE STAGG

PRINTER: Jesse Stagg   Wilcannia, Australia

JESSE STAGG

PRINTER: Jesse Stagg   Parkes, Australia

AOP ASSISTANTS' AWARDS

Landscapes, Interiors & Exteriors SERIES

ROB CADMAN

PRINTER: Rob Cadman

WINNER

SYSTEM OPERATOR: Rob Cadman

PEDRO ALVAREZ   MERIT

PRINTER: Pedro Alvarez

FRED HEWITT

PRINTER: Fred Hewitt

MERIT

SYSTEM OPERATOR: Fred Hewitt

| MEIKE NIXDORF | MERIT |

SYSTEM OPERATOR: Etizy digital artwork

DAVID OXBERRY

SYSTEM OPERATOR: David Oxberry

| ROB PAYNE

| GREG WHITE

| GREG WHITE

At bright, we are passionate about creativity. And in a world which appears to be consistently and worryingly controlled by procurement departments, cost-effectivity, economies and that is obsessed by savings (rather than added value), we want to bear a torch for originality, commissioned work and pushing things forward.

When it comes to photography, this starts with the assistants, without whom things just wouldn't happen. And who are going to be tomorrow's top-notch photographers. We totally support the AOP and the work that they do supporting the whole creative community, from the assistants to art buyers and established snappers alike. Long may creativity reign.

Still Life SINGLE

VERA KODAJOVA   **WINNER**

PRINTER: Vera Kodajova   SYSTEM OPERATOR: Steve Warner

SAM ARMSTRONG

PRINTER: Lupe Digital   SYSTEM OPERATOR: Sam Armstrong

SAM ARMSTRONG

PRINTER: Lupe Digital   SYSTEM OPERATOR: Sam Armstrong

DAVID OXBERRY

PRINTER: David Oxberry

Still Life SERIES

CHRIS JELLEY

PRINTER: Chris Jelley

MERIT

SYSTEM OPERATOR: Chris Jelley
Thanks to Carl Warner

PENNY COTTEE

PRINTER: Penny Cottee

Alvarez	Pedro	07966 524 161
Armstrong	Sam	07768 893 051
Cadman	Rob	0208 874 7102 / 07967 555 731
Cooper	Philippa	07966 152 517
Cottee	Penny	07770 433 322
Ferrari	Armando	07801 490700
Hewitt	Fred	07803 197 639
Jelley	Chris	07808 925 547
Kodajova	Vera	07900 218 460
Mallet	Peter	07932 994 638
Miller	Joel Micah	+49 711 507 6074
Nixdorf	Meike	+49 175 240 2704
Oxberry	David	07958 746 467
Padgham	Darren	+61 423 647 721
Payne	Rob	07818 435 552
Prince	Dan	07763 417 346
Robinson	Sam	07976 287 848
Stagg	Jesse	07798 800 468
Thompson	Paul	07887 604 833
Vasques	Luisa	07747 038 388
White	Greg	07769 586 525

BUTLER AND TANNER

Denmaur Papers plc

Denmaur Papers PLC
are delighted that their flagship product
Amadeus Silk has been selected for
Photography Awards 2005.
"Amadeus bringing images to Life"

WINTER & COMPANY
CULTURE IN COVERING

Proud to have contributed and be
associated with the awards

 BUTLER AND TANNER

Butler and Tanner specialises in producing high-quality books, catalogues and brochures for many of the world's leading companies. Butler and Tanner has also produced books of photography ranging from wildlife to fashion. Through its work with photo libraries, museums and galleries, Butler and Tanner regularly prints some of the world's most famous images.

In addition to conventional printing and binding, Butler and Tanner has also pioneered the use of digital printing for both personalised content and very short runs. The presses that Butler and Tanner uses for digital printing can print on the same stocks as litho and the results that it is achieving are indistinguishable from its conventional presses.

THE AOP WOULD LIKE TO THANK THE FOLLOWING
PEOPLE WHO HAVE GIVEN THEIR TIME, SKILL AND
EXPERTISE, AND THE MEMBERSHIP OF THE AOP
WHOSE SUPPORT MAKES THESE AWARDS POSSIBLE

PHOTOGRAPHY AWARDS 2005 JUDGES

ROBERT ALLEN
ANTHONY BLAKE
DAMON COLLINS
MIKE DENNY
ADRIAN EVANS
KELLIE FRENCH
JULIA FULLERTON-BATTEN
MARK GEORGE
HUGH GILBERT
MOLLY GODET
JOHN HEGARTY
JON LEVY
LEE MARTIN
PAUL MELLOR
ZED NELSON
KARENA PERRRONET-MILLER
PAUL REAS
MATTHEW RENTON
GRANT SMITH
NEIL SMITH
HOMER SYKES
KULBIR THANDI
SAMANTHA THOMAS
VALERIE HERSLEVEN

THANKS TO:

Tim Flach
Anthony Marsland
Nick Turpin
Dan Tierney

PHOTOGRAPHY AWARDS 2005 ORGANISERS

Nicola Waterhouse (Awards Manager)
Rachel Rogers (Publications &
Marketing Assistant)
Jonathan Briggs
(Acting Managing Director)
James McCarthy
(Website & Database Officer)

ADDITIONAL THANKS TO

Lassco for location shot.
www.lassco.co.uk

PHOTOGRAPHY AWARDS 2005 PHOTOGRAPHER

Nick Turpin is a street photographer:

'There is something about the making
of photographs in public places that
resonates with me more than any
other kind of photography. I think it
simply suits my personality. It's nice,
when taking pictures in the street,
not to have to participate in anyway
in the stream of life passing you by, it
makes me feel special to be there but
not to be chatting, not to be
shopping or not even to be heading
for somewhere else. I feel like I am
invisible to the passing crowds, this
in turn leads to a loss of my sense of
self which is the finest feeling of all.'

Represented by:
Balcony Jump Management
T: +44 (0)20 7831 3355
www.balconyjump.co.uk

kustom MOT MODELS

z | e | f | a | images

Alan	Mahon	020 7436 9020	235
Peter	Mallet	07932 994 638	284
Bob	Martin	07785 233 255	154
Leo	Mason	07831 467 926	147
Conor	Masterson	agent: 020 8675 3055	234
Toby	Maudsley	0208 870 3462	62
Mary-Jane	Maybury	07810 650 278	159, 263
Simon	McComb	0207 935 2626	57
Don	McPhee	020 7278 2332	261
Nadege	Meriau	0207 254 5476	17
	Metro Imaging	020 7865 0000	242
	Miles Calcraft Briginshaw Duffy	020 7073 6900	235
Joel Micah	Miller	0049 711 507 6074	285
Simon	Mills	0207 241 0088	63, 113
Dario	Mitidieri	0207 262 1774	138
Lars	Moeller	0045 20 113 322	148
Christopher	Morris	agent: 0033 147 055208	264
Kelvin	Murray	0207 431 5414	114
	Nail Communications	001 401 331 6245	238
	Naish Creative Imaging	020 7253 4440	250
Michael	Najjar	0049 302 1018286	247
Meike	Nixdorf	0049 175 240 2704	296, 306, 326
John	Offenbach	0207 249 4020	58, 88
	Ogilvy & Mather	020 7345 3000	222
Jonathan	Olley	07973 893 691	136, 164, 184
David	Oxberry	07958 746 467	328, 341
Darren	Padgham	0061 423 647 721	286
John	Parker	0207 229 8882	115
Sue	Parkhill	07711 579104	194
Rob	Payne	07818 435 552	287, 314, 330
Andrew	Pendlebury	0115 985 0680	18
Richard	Pohle	07850 947 132	129
Dan	Prince	07763 417 346	282
	Rainey Kelly Campbell Roalfe/Y & R	020 7404 2700	234
	Rankin Photography	020 7549 6805	222
Giles	Revell	0207 278 8818	50
Kiran	Ridley	07971 287 183	186
Reiner	Riedler	0043 6642 607960	262
Sam	Robinson	07976 287 848	288
John	Ross	0207 378 8080	242
	Saga. CG. SA	0032 2647 7643	231
Aliki	Sapountzi	0131 229 0951	188
David	Scheinmann	0207 636 2202	36
Morgan	Silk	0208 340 7633	98
Tim	Simmons	0207 729 0234	102
Sean	Smith	020 7278 2332	267
Jesse	Stagg	07798 800 468	289, 311, 315, 316
	Stanley's Post	020 7812 6154	224
David	Stewart	020 7608 2437	241
John	Stillwell	020 7963 7155	252
	Studio Myerscough	020 7689 0808	247, 248, 250
	TBWA Brussels	0032 2679 7511	231
Kulbir	Thandi	0207 403 0363	73
	The Guardian	020 7278 2332	261, 267
Paul	Thompson	07887 604 833	292
Simon	Thorpe	07966 261 532	26
Chippy	Tiffany	07850 540 701	75
	Time Magazine	020 7322 1150	253
	V.C.C.P	020 7802 5803	224
Luisa	Vasques	07747 038 388	300
Nick	Veasey	01622 737 722	40
Jaap	Vliegenthart	0031 20 411 7735	42
Richard	Wainwright	07797 718 769	130
Simon	Warmer	0031 20 692 3955	66
Greg	White	07769 586 525	332, 334
Lewis	Whyld	07815 820 323	161
Robert	Wilson	0207 263 9901	116
Julian	Wolkenstein	07748 735 858	76
Paul	Zak	07798 710710	232